FANCIES
VERSUS FADS

FANCIES
VERSUS FADS

G. K. CHESTERTON

CLETHAM CLASSICS

ERIS

265 Riverside Drive
New York, NY 10025

ISBN 978-1-916809-25-3

Cletham Classics is an innovative new range of
thoughtfully designed books comprising both
canonical texts and lesser-known works by
much-loved writers. Cletham's carefully select-
ed titles and dynamic visual style make for an
indispensable and ever-expanding collection.

eris.press/cletham-classics

TABLE OF CONTENTS

Fancies Versus Fads

INTRODUCTION

I have strung these things together on a slight
enough thread; but as the things themselves are
slight, it is possible that the thread (and the metaphor) may manage to hang together. These notes
range over very variegated topics and in many cases were made at very different times. They concern
all sorts of things from lady barristers to cave-men,
and from psycho-analysis to free verse. Yet they have
this amount of unity in their wandering, that they all
imply that it is only a more traditional spirit that is
truly able to wander. The wild theorists of our time
are quite unable to wander. When they talk of making new roads, they are only making new ruts. Each
of them is necessarily imprisoned in his own curious cosmos; in other words, he is limited by the very
largeness of his own generalization. The explanations
of the Marxian must not go outside economics; and
the student of Freud is forbidden to forget sex. To see
only the fanciful side of these serious sects may seem
a very frivolous pleasure; and I will not dispute that
these are very frivolous criticisms. I only submit that
this frivolity is the last lingering form of freedom.

In short, the note of these notes, so to speak, is that
it is only from a normal standpoint that all the nonsense of the world takes on something of the wild interest of wonderland. I mean it is only in the mirror of

a very moderate sense and sanity, which is all I have ever claimed to possess, that even insanities can appear as images clear enough to appeal to the imagination. After all, the ordinary orthodox person is he to whom the heresies can appear as fantasies. After all, it is we ordinary human and humdrum people who can enjoy eccentricity as a sort of elfland; while the eccentrics are too serious even to know that they are elves. When a man tells us that he disapproves of children being told fairy-tales, it is we who can perceive that he is himself a fairy. He himself has not the least idea of it. When he says he would discourage children from playing with tin soldiers, because it is militarism, it is we and not he who can enjoy in fancy the fantastic possibilities of his idea. It is we who suddenly think of children playing with little tin figures of philanthropists, rather round and with tin top-hats; the little tin gods of our commercial religion. It is we who develop his imaginative idea for him, by suggesting little leaden dolls of Conscientious Objectors in fixed attitudes of refined repugnance; or a whole regiment of tiny Quakers with little grey coats and white flags. He would never have thought of any of these substitutes for himself; his negation is purely negative. Or when an educational philosopher tells us that the child should have complete equality with the adult, he cannot really carry his idea any farther without our assistance. It will be from us and not from him that the natural suggestion will come; that the baby should take its turn and

G. K. CHESTERTON

carry the mother, the moment the mother is tired of carrying the baby. He will not, when left to himself, call up the poetical picture of the child wheeling a double perambulator with the father and mother at each end. He has no motive to look for lively logical developments; for him the assimilation of parent and child is simply a platitude; and an inevitable part of his own rather platitudinous philosophy. It is we and not he who can behold the whole vista and vanishing perspective of his own opinions; and work out what he really means. It is only those who have ordinary views who have extraordinary visions.

There is indeed nothing very extraordinary about these visions, except the extraordinary people who have provoked some of them. They are only a very sketchy sort of sketches of some of the strange things that may be found in the modern world. But however inadequate be the example, it is none the less true that this is the sound principle behind much better examples; and that, in those great things as in these small ones, sanity was the condition of satire. It is because Gulliver is a man of moderate stature that he can stray into the land of the giants and the land of the pygmies. It is Swift and not the professors of Laputa who sees the real romance of getting sunbeams out of cucumbers. It would be less than exact to call Swift a sunbeam in the house; but if he did not himself get much sunshine out of cucumbers, at least he let daylight into professors. It was not the mad Swift but the sane Swift who made that story so wild. The truth is more self-evident in men who were more sane. It is the good sense of Rabelais that makes him seem to grin like a gargoyle; and it is in a sense because Dickens was a Philistine that he saw the land so full of strange gods. These idle journalistic jottings have nothing in common with such standards of real literature, except the principle involved; but the principle is the right one.

But while these are frivolous essays, pretending only to touch on topics and theories they cannot exhaustively examine, I have added some that may not seem to fit so easily even into so slight a scheme. Nevertheless, they are in some sense connected with it. I have opened with an essay on rhyme, because it is a type of the sort of tradition which the anti-traditionalists now attack; and I have ended with one called "Milton and Merry England," because I feel that many may misunderstand my case against the new Puritans, if they have no notion of how I should attempt to meet the more accepted case in favour of the old Puritans. Both these articles appeared originally in the "London Mercury," and I desire to express my thanks to Mr. J. C. Squire for his kind permission to reprint them. But, in the latter case, I had the further feeling that I wished to express somewhere the historical sentiment that underlies the whole; the conviction that there did and does exist a more normal and national England, which we once inhabited and to which we may yet return; and which is not a Utopia but a home. I have therefore thought it worth

G. K. CHESTERTON

while to write this line of introduction to show that such a scrap-book is not entirely scrappy; and that even to touch such things lightly we need something like a test. It is necessary to have in hand a truth to judge modern philosophies rapidly; and it is necessary to judge them very rapidly to judge them before they disappear.

G. K. C.

THE ROMANCE OF RHYME

The poet in the comic opera, it will be remembered (I hope), claimed for his æsthetic authority that "Hey diddle diddle will rank as an idyll, if I pronounce it chaste." In face of a satire which still survives the fashion it satirized, it may require some moral courage seriously to pronounce it chaste, or to suggest that the nursery rhyme in question has really some of the qualities of an idyll. Of its chastity, in the vulgar sense, there need be little dispute, despite the scandal of the elopement of the dish with the spoon, which would seem as free from grossness as the loves of the triangles. And though the incident of the cow may have something of the moonstruck ecstasy of Endymion, that also has a silvery coldness about it worthy of the wilder aspects of Diana. The truth more seriously tenable is that this nursery rhyme is a complete and compact model of the nursery short story. The cow jumping over the moon fulfils to perfection the two essentials of such a story for children. It makes an effect that is fantastic out of objects that are familiar; and it makes a picture that is at once incredible and unmistakable. But it is yet more tenable, and here more to the point, that this nursery rhyme is emphatically a rhyme. Both the lilt and the jingle are just right for their purpose, and are worth whole libraries of elaborate literary verse for children. And the best proof of its vitality is that the satirist himself has unconsciously echoed the jingle even in making the joke. The metre of that nineteenth-century satire is the metre of the nursery rhyme. "Hey diddle diddle, the cat and the fiddle" and "Hey diddle diddle will rank as an idyll" are obviously both dancing to the same ancient tune; and that by no means the tune the old cow died of, but the more exhilarating air to which she jumped over the moon.

The whole history of the thing called rhyme can be found between those two things: the simple pleasure of rhyming "diddle" to "fiddle," and the more sophisticated pleasure of rhyming "diddle" to "idyll." Now the fatal mistake about poetry, and more than half of the fatal mistake about humanity, consists in forgetting that we should have the first kind of pleasure as well as the second. It might be said that we should have the first pleasure as the basis of the second; or yet more truly, the first pleasure inside the second. The fatal metaphor of progress, which means leaving things behind us, has utterly obscured the real idea of growth, which means leaving things inside us. The heart of the tree remains the same, however many rings are added to it; and a man cannot leave his heart behind by running hard with his legs. In the core of all culture are the things that may be said, in every sense, to be learned by heart. In the innermost part of all poetry is the nursery rhyme, the nonsense that is too happy even to care about being nonsensical. It

G. K. CHESTERTON

may lead on to the more elaborate nonsense of the Gilbertian line, or even the far less poetic nonsense of some of the Browningesque rhymes. But the true enjoyment of poetry is always in having the simple pleasure as well as the subtle pleasure. Indeed it is on this primary point that so many of our artistic and other reforms seem to go wrong. What is the matter with the modern world is that it is trying to get simplicity in everything except the soul. Where the soul really has simplicity it can be grateful for anything—even complexity. Many peasants have to be vegetarians, and their ordinary life is really a simple life. But the peasants do not despise a good dinner when they can get it; they wolf it down with enthusiasm, because they have not only the simple life but the simple spirit. And it is so with the modern modes of art which revert, very rightly, to what is "primitive." But their moral mistake is that they try to combine the ruggedness that should belong to simplicity with a superciliousness that should only belong to satiety. The last Futurist draughtsmanship, for instance, evidently has the aim of drawing a tree as it might be drawn by a child of ten. I think the new artists would admit it; nor do I merely sneer at it. I am willing to admit, especially for the sake of argument, that there is a truth of philosophy and psychology in this attempt to attain the clarity even through the crudity of childhood. In this sense I can see what a man is driving at when he draws a tree merely as a stick with smaller sticks standing out of it. He may be trying to trace in black and white or grey a primeval and almost prenatal illumination; that it is very remarkable that a stick should exist, and still more remarkable that a stick should stick up or stick out. He may be similarly enchanted with his own stick of charcoal or grey chalk; he may be enraptured, as a child is, with the mere fact that it makes a mark on the paper—a highly poetic fact in itself. But the child does not despise the real tree for being different from his drawing of the tree. He does not despise Uncle Humphrey because that talented amateur can really draw a tree. He does not think less of the real sticks because they are live sticks, and can grow and branch and curve in a way uncommon in walking-sticks. Because he has a single eye he can enjoy a double pleasure. This distinction, which seems strangely neglected, may be traced again in the drama and most other domains of art. Reformers insist that the audiences of simpler ages were content with bare boards or rudimentary scenery if they could hear Sophocles or Shakespeare talking a language of the gods. They were very properly contented with plain boards. But they were not discontented with pageants. The people who appreciated Antony's oration as such would have appreciated Aladdin's palace as such. They did not think gilding and spangles substitutes for poetry and philosophy, because they are not. But they did think gilding and spangles great and admirable gifts of God, because they are.

G. K. CHESTERTON

But the application of this distinction here is to the case of rhyme in poetry. And the application of it is that we should never be ashamed of enjoying a thing as a rhyme as well as enjoying it as a poem. And I think the modern poets who try to escape from the rhyming pleasure, in pursuit of a freer poetical pleasure, are making the same fundamentally fallacious attempt to combine simplicity with superiority. Such a poet is like a child who could take no pleasure in a tree because it looked like a tree, or a playgoer who could take no pleasure in the Forest of Arden because it looked like a forest. It is not impossible to find a sort of prig who professes that he could listen to literature in any scenery, but strongly objects to good scenery. And in poetical criticism and creation there has also appeared the prig who insists that any new poem must avoid the sort of melody that makes the beauty of any old song. Poets must put away childish things, including the child's pleasure in the mere sing-song of irrational rhyme. It may be hinted that when poets put away childish things they will put away poetry. But it may be well to say a word in further justification of rhyme as well as poetry, in the child as well as the poet. Now, the neglect of this nursery instinct would be a blunder, even if it were merely an animal instinct or an automatic instinct. If a rhyme were to a man merely what a bark is to a dog, or a crow to a cock, it would be clear that such natural things cannot be merely neglected. It is clear that a canine epic, about Argus instead of Ulysses, would have a beat ultimately consisting of barks. It is clear that a long poem like "Chantecler," written by a real cock, would be to the tune of Cock-a-doodle-doo. But in truth the nursery rhyme has a nobler origin; if it be ancestral it is not animal; its principle is a primary one, not only in the body but in the soul.

Milton prefaced "Paradise Lost" with a ponderous condemnation of rhyme. And perhaps the finest and even the most familiar line in the whole of "Paradise Lost" is really a glorification of rhyme. "Seasons return, but not to me return," is not only an echo that has all the ring of rhyme in its form, but it happens to contain nearly all the philosophy of rhyme in its spirit. The wonderful word "return" has, not only in its sound but in its sense, a hint of the whole secret of song. It is not merely that its very form is a fine example of a certain quality in English, somewhat similar to that which Mrs. Meynell admirably analysed in one of her last beautiful essays, in the case of words like "unforgiven." It is that it describes poetry itself, not only in a mechanical but a moral sense. Song is not only a recurrence, it is a return. It does not merely, like the child in the nursery, take pleasure in seeing the wheels go round. It also wishes to go back as well as round; to go back to the nursery where such pleasures are found. Or to vary the metaphor slightly, it does not merely rejoice in the rotation of a wheel on the road, as if it were a fixed wheel in the air. It is not only the wheel but the wagon that is returning. That labouring caravan is always travelling

G. K. CHESTERTON

towards some camping-ground that it has lost and cannot find again. No lover of poetry needs to be told that all poems are full of that noise of returning wheels; and none more than the poems of Milton himself. The whole truth is obvious, not merely in the poem, but even in the two words of the title. All poems might be bound in one book under the title of "Paradise Lost." And the only object of writing "Paradise Lost" is to turn it, if only by a magic and momentary illusion, into "Paradise Regained."

It is in this deeper significance of return that we must seek for the peculiar power in the recurrence we call rhyme. It would be easy enough to reply to Milton's strictures on rhyme in the spirit of a sensible if superficial liberality by saying that it takes all sorts to make a world, and especially the world of the poets. It is evident enough that Milton might have been right to dispense with rhyme without being right to despise it. It is obvious that the peculiar dignity of his religious epic would have been weakened if it had been a rhymed epic, beginning:

Of man's first disobedience and the fruit
Of that forbidden tree whose mortal root.

But it is equally obvious that Milton himself would not have tripped on the light fantastic toe with quite so much charm and cheerfulness in the lines:

But come thou Goddess fair and free

if the goddess had been yclept something else, as, for the sake of argument, Syrinx. Milton in his more reasonable moods would have allowed rhyme in theory a place in all poetry, as he allowed it in practice in his own poetry. But he would certainly have said at this time, and possibly at all times, that he allowed it an inferior place, or at least a secondary place. But is its place secondary; and is it in any sense inferior?

The romance of rhyme does not consist merely in the pleasure of a jingle, though this is a pleasure of which no man should be ashamed. Certainly most men take pleasure in it, whether or not they are ashamed of it. We see it in the older fashion of prolonging the chorus of a song with syllables like "rumty tumty" or "tooral looral." We see it in the similar but later fashion of discussing whether a truth is objective or subjective, or whether a reform is constructive or destructive, or whether an argument is deductive or inductive: all bearing witness to a very natural love for those nursery rhyme recurrences which make a sort of song without words, or at least without any kind of intellectual significance. But something much deeper is involved in the love of rhyme as distinct from other poetic forms, something which is perhaps too deep and subtle to be described. The nearest approximation to the truth I can think of is something like this: that while all forms of genuine verse recur, there is in rhyme a sense of return to exactly the same place.

All modes of song go forward and backward like the tides of the sea; but in the great sea of Homeric or Virgilian hexameters, the sea that carried the labouring ships of Ulysses and Æneas, the thunder of the breakers is rhythmic, but the margin of the foam is necessarily irregular and vague. In rhyme there is rather a sense of water poured safely into one familiar well, or (to use a nobler metaphor) of ale poured safely into one familiar flagon. The armies of Homer and Virgil advance and retreat over a vast country, and suggest vast and very profound sentiments about it, about whether it is their own country or only a strange country. But when the old nameless ballad boldly rhymes "the bonny ivy tree" to "my ain countree" the vision at once dwindles and sharpens to a very vivid image of a single soldier passing under the ivy that darkens his own door. Rhythm deals with similarity, but rhyme with identity. Now in the one word identity are involved perhaps the deepest and certainly the dearest human things. He who is homesick does not desire houses or even homes. He who is love-sick does not want to see all the women with whom he might have fallen in love. Only he who is sea-sick, perhaps, may be said to have a cosmopolitan craving for all lands or any kind of land. And this is probably why sea-sickness, like cosmopolitanism, has never yet been a high inspiration to song.

Songs, especially the most poignant of them, generally refer to some absolute, to some positive place or person for whom no similarity is a substitute. In such a case all approximation is merely asymptotic. The prodigal returns to his father's house and not the house next door, unless he is still an imperfectly sober prodigal. The lover desires his lady and not her twin sister, except in old complications of romance. And even the spiritualist is generally looking for a ghost and not merely for ghosts. I think the intolerable torture of spiritualism must be a doubt about identity. Anyhow, it will generally be found that where this call for the identical has been uttered most ringingly and unmistakably in literature, it has been uttered in rhyme. Another purpose for which this pointed and definite form is very much fitted is the expression of dogma, as distinct from doubt or even opinion. This is why, with all allowance for a decline in the most classical effects of the classical tongue, the rhymed Latin of the mediæval hymns does express what it had to express in a very poignant poetical manner, as compared with the reverent agnosticism so nobly uttered in the rolling unrhymed metres of the ancients. For even if we regard the matter of the mediæval verses as a dream, it was at least a vivid dream, a dream full of faces, a dream of love and of lost things. And something of the same spirit runs in a vaguer way through proverbs and phrases that are not exactly religious, but rather in a rude sense philosophical, but which all move with the burden of returning; things to be felt only in familiar fragments ... *on revient toujours* ... it's the old story ... it's love that makes the world go round; and

G. K. CHESTERTON

all roads lead to Rome: we might almost say that all roads lead to Rhyme.

Milton's revolt against rhyme must be read in the light of history. Milton is the Renascence frozen into a Puritan form; the beginning of a period which was in a sense classic, but was in a still more definite sense aristocratic. There the Classicist was the artistic aristocrat because the Calvinist was the spiritual aristocrat. The seventeenth century was intensely individualistic; it had both in the noble and the ignoble sense a respect for persons. It had no respect whatever for popular traditions; and it was in the midst of its purely logical and legal excitement that most of the popular traditions died. The Parliament appeared and the people disappeared. The arts were put under patrons, where they had once been under patron saints. The English schools and colleges at once strengthened and narrowed the New Learning, making it something rather peculiar to one country and one class. A few men talked a great deal of good Latin, where all men had once talked a little bad Latin. But they talked even the good Latin so that no Latinist in the world could understand them. They confined all study of the classics to that of the most classical period, and grossly exaggerated the barbarity and barrenness of patristic Greek or mediæval Latin. It is as if a man said that because the English translation of the Bible is perhaps the best English in the world, therefore Addison and Pater and Newman are not worth reading. We can imagine what men in such a mood would have said of the rude rhymed hexameters of the monks; and it is not unnatural that they should have felt a reaction against rhyme itself. For the history of rhyme is the history of something else, very vast and sometimes invisible, certainly somewhat indefinable, against which they were in aristocratic rebellion.

That thing is difficult to define in impartial modern terms. It might well be called Romance, and that even in a more technical sense, since it corresponds to the rise of the Romance languages as distinct from the Roman language. It might more truly be called Religion, for historically it was the gradual re-emergence of Europe through the Dark Ages, because it still had one religion, though no longer one rule. It was, in short, the creation of Christendom. It may be called Legend, for it is true that the most overpowering presence in it is that of omni-present and powerful popular Legend; so that things that may never have happened, or, as some say, could never have happened, are nevertheless rooted in our racial memory like things that have happened to ourselves. The whole Arthurian Cycle, for instance, seems something more real than reality. If the faces in that darkness of the Dark Ages, Lancelot and Arthur and Merlin and Modred, are indeed faces in a dream, they are like faces in a real dream: a dream in a bed and not a dream in a book. Subconsciously at least, I should be much less surprised if Arthur was to come again than I should be if the Superman were to come at all. Again, the thing might be called Gossip:

G. K. CHESTERTON

a noble name, having in it the name of God and one of the most generous and genial of the relations of men. For I suppose there has seldom been a time when such a mass of culture and good traditions of craft and song have been handed down orally, by one universal buzz of conversation, through centuries of ignorance down to centuries of greater knowledge. Education must have been an eternal *viva voce* examination; but the men passed their examination. At least they went out in such rude sense masters of art as to create the Song of Roland and the round Roman arches that carry the weight of so many Gothic towers. Finally, of course, it can be called ignorance, barbarism, black superstition, a reaction towards obscurantism and old night; and such a view is eminently complete and satisfactory, only that it leaves behind it a sort of weak wonder as to why the very youngest poets do still go on writing poems about the sword of Arthur and the horn of Roland.

All this was but the beginning of a process which has two great points of interest. The first is the way in which the mediæval movement did rebuild the old Roman civilization; the other was the way in which it did not. A strange interest attaches to the things which had never existed in the pagan culture and did appear in the Christian culture. I think it is true of most of them that they had a quality that can very approximately be described as popular, or perhaps as vulgar, as indeed we still talk of the languages which at that time liberated themselves from Latin as the vulgar tongues. And to many Classicists these things would appear to be vulgar in a more vulgar sense. They were vulgar in the sense of being vivid almost to excess, of making a very direct and unsophisticated appeal to the emotions. The first law of heraldry was to wear the heart upon the sleeve. Such mediævalism was the reverse of mere mysticism, in the sense of mere mystery; it might more truly be described as sensationalism. One of these things, for instance, was a hot and even an impatient love of colour. It learned to paint before it could draw, and could afford the twopence coloured long before it could manage the penny plain. It culminated at last, of course, in the energy and gaiety of the Gothic; but even the richness of Gothic rested on a certain psychological simplicity. We can contrast it with the classic by noting its popular passion for telling a story in stone. We may admit that a Doric portico is a poem, but no one would describe it as an anecdote. The time was to come when much of the imagery of the cathedrals was to be lost; but it would have mattered the less that it was defaced by its enemies if it had not been already neglected by its friends. It would have mattered less if the whole tide of taste among the rich had not turned against the old popular masterpieces. The Puritans defaced them, but the Cavaliers did not truly defend them. The Cavaliers were also aristocrats of the new classical culture, and used the word Gothic in the sense of barbaric. For the benefit of the Teutonists we may

G. K. CHESTERTON

note in parenthesis that, if this phrase meant that Gothic was despised, it also meant that the Goths were despised. But when the Cavaliers came back, after the Puritan interregnum, they restored not in the style of Pugin but in the style of Wren. The very thing we call the Restoration, which was the restoration of King Charles, was also the restoration of St. Paul's. And it was a very modern restoration.

So far we might say that simple people do not like simple things. This is certainly true if we compare the classic with these highly coloured things of mediævalism, or all the vivid visions which first began to glow in the night of the Dark Ages. Now one of these things was the romantic expedient called rhyme. And even in this, if we compare the two, we shall see something of the same paradox by which the simple like complexities and the complex like simplicities. The ignorant liked rich carvings and melodious and often ingenious rhymes. The learned liked bare walls and blank verse. But in the case of rhyme it is peculiarly difficult to define the double and yet very definite truth. It is difficult to define the sense in which rhyme is artificial and the sense in which it is simple. In truth it is simple because it is artificial. It is an artifice of the kind enjoyed by children and other poetic people; it is a toy. As a technical accomplishment it stands at the same distance from the popular experience as the old popular sports. Like swimming, like dancing, like drawing the bow, anybody can do it, but nobody can do it without taking the trouble to do it; and only a few can do it very well. In a hundred ways it was akin to that simple and even humble energy that made all the lost glory of the guilds. Thus their rhyme was useful as well as ornamental. It was not merely a melody but also a mnemonic; just as their towers were not merely trophies but beacons and belfries. In another aspect rhyme is akin to rhetoric, but of a very positive and emphatic sort: the coincidence of sound giving the effect of saying, "It is certainly so." Shakespeare realized this when he rounded off a fierce or romantic scene with a rhymed couplet. I know that some critics do not like this, but I think there is a moment when a drama ought to become a melodrama. Then there is a much older effect of rhyme that can only be called mystical, which may seem the very opposite of the utilitarian, and almost equally remote from the rhetorical. Yet it shares with the former the tough texture of something not easily forgotten, and with the latter the touch of authority which is the aim of all oratory. The thing I mean may be found in the fact that so many of the old proverbial prophecies, from Merlin to Mother Shipton, were handed down in rhyme. It can be found in the very name of Thomas the Rhymer.

But the simplest way of putting this popular quality is in a single word: it is a song. Rhyme corresponds to a melody so simple that it goes straight like an arrow to the heart. It corresponds to a chorus so familiar and obvious that all men can join in it. I am not disturbed by the suggestion that such an arrow

G. K. CHESTERTON

of song, when it hits the heart, may entirely miss the head. I am not concerned to deny that the chorus may sometimes be a drunken chorus, in which men have lost their heads to find their tongues. I am not defending but defining; I am trying to find words for a large but elusive distinction between certain things that are certainly poetry and certain other things which are also song. Of course it is only an accident that Horace opens his greatest series of odes by saying that he detests the profane populace and wishes to drive them from his temple of poetry. But it is the sort of accident that is almost an allegory. There is even a sense in which it has a practical side. When all is said, *could* a whole crowd of men sing the "Descende Cœlo," that noble ode, as a crowd can certainly sing the "Dies Irae," or for that matter "Down among the Dead Men"? Did Horace himself sing the Horatian odes in the sense in which Shakespeare could sing, or could hardly help singing, the Shakespearean songs? I do not know, having no kind of scholarship on these points. But I do not feel that it could have been at all the same thing; and my only purpose is to attempt a rude description of that thing. Rhyme is consonant to the particular kind of song that can be a popular song, whether pathetic or passionate or comic; and Milton is entitled to his true distinction; nobody is likely to sing "Paradise Lost" as if it were a song of that kind. I have tried to suggest my sympathy with rhyme, in terms true enough to be accepted by the other side as expressing their antipathy for it. I have admitted that rhyme is a toy and even a trick, of the sort that delights children. I have admitted that every rhyme is a nursery rhyme. What I will never admit is that anyone who is too big for the nursery is big enough for the Kingdom of God, though the God were only Apollo.

A good critic should be like God in the great saying of a Scottish mystic. George Macdonald said that God was easy to please and hard to satisfy. That paradox is the poise of all good artistic appreciation. Without the first part of the paradox appreciation perishes, because it loses the power to appreciate. Good criticism, I repeat, combines the subtle pleasure in a thing being done well with the simple pleasure in it being done at all. It combines the pleasure of the scientific engineer in seeing how the wheels work together to a logical end with the pleasure of the baby in seeing the wheels go round. It combines the pleasure of the artistic draughtsman in the fact that his lines of charcoal, light and apparently loose, fall exactly right and in a perfect relation with the pleasure of the child in the fact that the charcoal makes marks of any kind on the paper. And in the same fashion it combines the critic's pleasure in a poem with the child's pleasure in a rhyme. The historical point about this kind of poetry, the rhymed romantic kind, is that it rose out of the Dark Ages with the whole of this huge popular power behind it, the human love of a song, a riddle, a proverb, a pun or a nursery rhyme; the sing-song of innumerable

G. K. CHESTERTON

children's games, the chorus of a thousand camp-fires and a thousand taverns. When poetry loses its link with all these people who are easily pleased it loses all its power of giving pleasure. When a poet looks down on a rhyme it is, I will not say as if he looked down on a daisy (which might seem possible to the more literal-minded), but rather as if he looked down on a lark because he had been up in a balloon. It is cutting away the very roots of poetry; it is revolting against nature because it is natural, against sunshine because it is bright, or mountains because they are high, or moonrise because it is mysterious. The freezing process began after the Reformation with a fastidious search for finer yet freer forms; to-day it has ended in formlessness.

But the joke of it is that even when it is formless it is still fastidious. The new anarchic artists are not ready to accept everything. They are not ready to accept anything except anarchy. Unless it observes the very latest conventions of unconventionality, they would rule out anything classic as coldly as any classic ever ruled out anything romantic. But the classic was a form; and there was even a time when it was a new form. The men who invented Sapphics did invent a new metre; the introduction of Elizabethan blank verse was a real revolution in literary form. But *vers libre*, or nine-tenths of it, is not a new metre any more than sleeping in a ditch is a new school of architecture. It is no more a revolution in literary form than eating meat raw is an innovation in cookery.

It is not even original, because it is not creative; the artist does not invent anything, but only abolishes something. But the only point about it that is to my present purpose is expressed in the word "pride." It is not merely proud in the sense of being exultant, but proud in the sense of being disdainful. Such outlaws are more exclusive than aristocrats; and their anarchical arrogance goes far beyond the pride of Milton and the aristocrats of the New Learning. And this final refinement has completed the work which the saner aristocrats began, the work now most evident in the world: the separation of art from the people. I need not insist on the sensational and self-evident character of that separation. I need not recommend the modern poet to attempt to sing his *vers libres* in a public house. I need not even urge the young Imagist to read out a number of his disconnected Images to a public meeting. The thing is not only admitted but admired. The old artist remained proud in spite of his unpopularity; the new artist is proud because of his unpopularity; perhaps it is his chief ground for pride.

Dwelling as I do in the Dark Ages, or at latest among the mediæval fairy-tales, I am yet moved to remember something I once read in a modern fairy-tale. As it happens, I have already used the name of George Macdonald; and in the best of his books there is a description of how a young miner in the mountains could always drive away the subterranean goblins if he could remember and repeat any kind of rhyme. The impromptu rhymes were often doggerel, as was the dog-Latin of many monkish hexameters or the burden of many rude Border ballads. But I have a notion that they drove away the devils, blue devils of pessimism and black devils of pride. Anyhow Madame Montessori, who has apparently been deploring the educational effects of fairy-tales, would probably see in me a pitiable example of such early perversion, for that image which was one of my first impressions seems likely enough to be one of my last; and when the noise of many new and original musical instruments, with strange shapes and still stranger noises, has passed away like a procession, I shall hear in the succeeding silence only a rustle and scramble among the rocks and a boy singing on the mountain.

HAMLET AND THE PSYCHOANALYST

This morning, for a long stretch of hours before breakfast, and even as it were merging into breakfast, and almost overlapping breakfast, I was engaged in scientific researches in the great new department of psycho-analysis. Every journalist knows by this time that psycho-analysis largely depends on the study of dreams. But in order to study our dreams it is necessary to dream; and in order to dream it is necessary to sleep. So, while others threw away the golden hours in lighter and less learned occupations, while ignorant and superstitious peasants were already digging in their ignorant and superstitious kitchen-gardens, to produce their ignorant and superstitious beans and potatoes, while priests were performing their pious mummeries and poets composing lyrics on listening to the skylark—I myself was pioneering hundreds of years ahead of this benighted century; ruthlessly and progressively probing into all the various horrible nightmares, from which a happier future will take its oracles and its commandments. I will not describe my dreams in detail; I am not quite so ruthless a psychologist as all that. And indeed it strikes me as possible that the new psychologist will be rather a bore at breakfast. My dream was something about wandering in some sort of catacombs under the Albert Hall, and it involved eating jumbles (a brown flexible cake now almost gone from us, like so many glories of England) and also arguing with a Theosophist. I cannot fit this in very well with Freud and his theory of suppressed impulses. For I swear I never in my life suppressed the impulse to eat a jumble or to argue with a Theosophist. And as for wandering about in the Albert Hall, nobody could ever have had an impulse to do that.

When I came down to breakfast I looked at the morning paper; not (as you humorously suggest) at the evening paper. I had not pursued my scientific studies quite so earnestly as that. I looked at the morning paper, as I say, and found it contained a good deal about Psycho-Analysis, indeed it explained almost everything about Psycho-Analysis except what it was. This was naturally a thing which newspapers would present in a rather fragmentary fashion; and I fitted the fragments together as best I could. Apparently the dreams were merely symbols; and apparently symbols of something very savage and horrible which remained a secret. This seems to me a highly unscientific use of the word symbol. A symbol is not a disguise but rather a display; the best expression of something that cannot otherwise be expressed. Eating a jumble may mean that I wished to bite off my father's nose (the mother-complex being strong on me); but it does not seem to show much symbolic talent. The Albert Hall may imply the murder of an uncle; but it hardly makes itself very clear. And we do not seem to be getting much nearer the

G. K. CHESTERTON

truth by dreaming, if we hide things by night more completely than we repress them by day. Anyhow, the murdered uncle reminds me of Hamlet, of whom more anon; at the moment I am merely remarking that my newspaper was a little vague; and I was all the more relieved to open my "London Mercury" and find an article on the subject by so able and suggestive a writer as Mr. J. D. Beresford.

Mr. J. D. Beresford practically asked himself whether he should become a psycho-analyst or continue to be a novelist. It will readily be understood that he did not put it precisely in these words; he would probably put psycho-analysis higher, and very possibly his own fiction lower; for men of genius are often innocent enough of their own genuine originality. That is a form of the unconscious mind with which none of us will quarrel. But I have no desire to watch a man of genius tying himself in knots, and perhaps dying in agony, in the attempt to be conscious of his own unconsciousness. I have seen too many unfortunate sceptics thus committing suicide by self-contradiction. Haeckel and his Determinists, in my youth, bullied us all about the urgent necessity of choosing a philosophy which would prove the impossibility of choosing anything. No doubt the new psychology will somehow enable us to know what we are doing, about all that we do without knowing it. These things come and go, and pass through their phases in order, from the time when they are as experimental as Freudism to the time when they are as exploded as Darwinism. But I never can understand men allowing things so visibly fugitive to hide things that are visibly permanent, like morals and religion and (what is in question here) the art of letters. *Ars longa, scientia brevis.*

Anyhow, as has been said, psycho-analysis depends in practice upon the interpretation of dreams. I do not know whether making masses of people, chiefly children, confess their dreams, would lead to a great output of literature; though it would certainly lead, if I know anything of human nature, to a glorious output of lies. There is something touching in the in-human innocence of the psychologist, who is already talking of the scientific exactitude of results reached by the one particular sort of evidence that cannot conceivably be checked or tested in any way whatever. But, as Mr. Beresford truly says, the general notion of finding signs in dreams is as old as the world; but even the special theory of it is older than many seem to suppose. Indeed, it is not only old, but obvious; and was never discovered, because it was always noticed. Long before the present fashion I myself (who, heaven knows, am no psychologist) remember saying that as there is truth in all popular traditions, there is truth in the popular saying that dreams go by the rule of contraries. That is, that a man does often think at night about the very things he does not think by day. But the popular saying had in it a certain virtue never found in the anti-popular sciences of our day. Popular superstition has one enormous

G. K. CHESTERTON

element of sanity; it is never serious. We talk of ages like the mediæval as the ages of faith; but it would be quite as true a tribute to call them the ages of doubt; of a healthy doubt, and even a healthy derision. There was always something more or less consciously grotesque about an old ghost story. There was fun mixed with the fear; and the yokels knew too much about turnips not occasionally to think of turnip-ghosts. There is no fun about psycho-analysis. One yokel would say, "Ar, they do say dreams go by contraries." And then the others would say "Ar," and they would all laugh in a deep internal fashion. But when Mr. J. D. Beresford says that Freud's theory is among scientific theories the most attractive for novelists, "it was a theory of sex, the all but universal theme of the novel," it is clear that our audience is slower and more solemn than the yokels. For nobody laughs at all. People seem to have lost the power of reacting to the humorous stimulus. When one milkmaid dreamed of a funeral, the other milkmaid said, "That means a wedding," and then they would both giggle. But when Mr. J. D. Beresford says that the theory "adumbrated the suggestion of a freer morality, by dwelling upon the physical and spiritual necessity for the liberation of impulse," the point seems somehow to be missed. Not a single giggle is heard in the deep and disappointing silence. It seems truly strange that when a modern and brilliant artist actually provides jokes far more truly humorous than the rude jests of the yokels and the milkmaids, the finer effort should meet with the feebler response. It is but an example of the unnatural solemnity, like an artificial vacuum, in which all these modern experiments are conducted. But no doubt if Freud had enjoyed the opportunity of explaining his ideas in an ancient ale-house, they would have met with more spontaneous applause.

I hope I do not seem unsympathetic with Mr. Beresford; for I not only admire his talent, but I am at this moment acting in strict obedience to his theories. I am—I say it proudly—acting as a disciple of Freud, who apparently forbids me to conceal any impulse, presumably including the impulse to laugh. I mean no disrespect to Mr. Beresford; but my first duty, of course, is to my own psychological inside. And goodness knows what damage might not be done to the most delicate workings of my own mental apparatus (as Mr. Arnold Bennett called it) if I were to subject it to the sudden and violent strain of not smiling at the scientific theory which is attractive because it is sexual, or of forcing my features into a frightful composure when I hear of the spiritual necessity for the liberation of impulse. I am not quite sure how far the liberation of impulse is to be carried out in practice by its exponents in theory; I do not know whether it is better to liberate the impulse to throw somebody else out of an express train in order to have the carriage to oneself all the way; or what may be the penalties for repressing the native instinct to shoot Mr. Lloyd George. But obviously the greater includes the

G. K. CHESTERTON

less; and it would be very illogical if we were allowed to chuck out our fellow-traveller but not to chaff him; or if I were permitted to shoot at Mr. George but not to smile at Mr. Beresford. And though I am not so serious as he is, I assure him that in this I am quite as sincere as he is. In that sense I do seriously regret his seriousness; I do seriously think such seriousness a very serious evil. For some healthy human impulses are really the better for the relief by words and gestures, and one of them is the universal human sense that there is something comic about the relations of the sexes. The impulse to laugh at the mention of morality as "free" or of sex science as "attractive" is one of the impulses which is already gratified by most people who have never heard of psycho-analysis and is only mortified by people like the psycho-analysts.

Mr. Beresford must therefore excuse me if, with a sincere desire to follow his serious argument seriously, I note at the beginning a certain normal element of comedy of which critics of his school seem to be rather unconscious. When he asks whether this theory of the nemesis of suppression can serve the purposes of great literary work, it would seem natural at first to test it by the example of the greatest literary works. And, judged by this scientific test, it must be admitted that our literary classics would appear to fail. Lady Macbeth does not suffer as a sleep-walker because she has resisted the impulse to murder Duncan, but rather (by some curious trick of thought) because she has yielded to it. Hamlet's uncle is in a morbid frame of mind, not, as one would naturally expect, because he had thwarted his own development by leaving his own brother alive and in possession; but actually because he has triumphantly liberated himself from the morbid impulse to pour poison in his brother's ear. On the theory of psycho-analysis, as expounded, a man ought to be haunted by the ghosts of all the men he has not murdered. Even if they were limited to those he has felt a vague fancy for murdering, they might make a respectable crowd to follow at his heels. Yet Shakespeare certainly seems to represent Macbeth as haunted by Banquo, whom he removed at one blow from the light of the sun and from his own subconsciousness. Hell ought to mean the regret for lost opportunities for crime; the insupportable thought of houses still standing unburned or unburgled, or of wealthy uncles still walking about alive with their projecting watch-chains. Yet Dante certainly seemed to represent it as concerned exclusively with things done and done with, and not as merely the morbidly congested imagination of a thief who had not thieved and a murderer who had not murdered. In short, it is only too apparent that the poets and sages of the past knew very little of psycho-analysis, and whether or no Mr. Beresford can achieve great literary effects with it, they managed to achieve their literary effects without it. This is but a preliminary point, and I shall touch the more serious problem in a few minutes, if the fashion has not changed before then. For the moment I only take

        G. K. CHESTERTON

the test of literary experience, and of how independent of such theories have been the real masterpieces of man. Men are still excited over the poetic parts of poets like Shakespeare and Dante; if they go to sleep it is over the scientific parts. It is over some system of the spheres which Dante thought the very latest astronomy, or some argument about the humours of the body which Shakespeare thought the very latest physiology. I appeal to Mr. Beresford's indestructible sense of humanity and his still undestroyed sense of humour. What would have become of the work of Dickens if it had been rewritten to illustrate the thesis of Darwin? What even of the work of Mr. Kipling if modified to meet the theories of Mr. Kidd? Believe me, the proportions are as I have said. Art is long, but science is fleeting; and Mr. Beresford's subconsciousness, though stout and brave, is in danger of being not so much a muffled drum as a drum which somebody silences for ever; by knocking a hole in it, only to find nothing inside. But there is one incidental moral in the matter that seems to me topical and rather arresting. It concerns the idea of punishment. The psycho-analysts continue to buzz in a mysterious manner round the problem of Hamlet. They are especially interested in the things of which Hamlet was unconscious, not to mention the things of which Shakespeare was unconscious. It is in vain for old-fashioned rationalists like myself to point out that this is like dissecting the brain of Puck or revealing the real private life of Punch and Judy. The discussion no longer revolves round whether Hamlet is mad, but whether everybody is mad, especially the experts investigating the madness. And the curious thing about this process is that even when the critics are really subtle enough to see subtle things, they are never simple enough to see self-evident things. A really fine critic is reported as arguing that in Hamlet the consciousness willed one thing and the subconsciousness another. Apparently the conscious Hamlet had unreservedly embraced and even welcomed the obligation of vengeance, but the shock (we are told) had rendered the whole subject painful, and started a strange and secret aversion to the scheme. It did not seem to occur to the writers that there might possibly be something slightly painful, at the best, in cutting the throat of your own uncle and the husband of your own mother. There might certainly be an aversion from the act; but I do not quite see why it should be an unconscious aversion. It seems just possible that a man might be quite conscious of not liking such a job. Where he differed from the modern morality was that he believed in the possibility of disliking it and yet doing it.

But to follow the argument of these critics, one would think that murdering the head of one's family was a sort of family festivity or family joke; a gay and innocent indulgence into which the young prince would naturally have thrown himself with thoughtless exuberance, were it not for the dark and secretive thoughts that had given him an unaccountable

G. K. CHESTERTON

distaste for it. Suppose it were borne in upon one of these modern middle-class critics, of my own rank and routine of life (possibly through his confidence in the messages at a Spiritualist séance) that it was his business to go home to Brompton or Surbiton and stick the carving-knife into Uncle William, who had poisoned somebody and was beyond the reach of the law. It is possible that the critic's first thought would be that it was a happy way of spending a half-holiday; and that only in the critic's subconsciousness the suspicion would stir that there was something unhappy about the whole business. But it seems also possible that the regret might not be confined to his subconsciousness, but might swim almost to the surface of his consciousness. In plain words, this sort of criticism has lost the last rags of common sense. Hamlet requires no such subconscious explanation, for he explains himself, and was perhaps rather too fond of doing so. He was a man to whom duty had come in a very dreadful and repulsive form, and to a man not fitted for that form of duty. There was a conflict, but he was conscious of it from beginning to end. He was not an unconscious person; but a far too conscious one.

Strangely enough, this theory of subconscious repulsion in the dramatic character is itself an example of subconscious repulsion in the modern critic. It is the critic who has a sort of subliminal prejudice which makes him avoid something, that seems very simple to others. The thing which he secretly and obscurely avoids, from the start, is the very simple fact of the morality in which Shakespeare did believe, as distinct from all the crude psychology in which he almost certainly did not believe. Shakespeare certainly did believe in the struggle between duty and inclination. The critic instinctively avoids the admission that Hamlet's was a struggle between duty and inclination; and tries to substitute a struggle between consciousness and subconsciousness. He gives Hamlet a complex to avoid giving him a conscience. But he is actually forced to talk as if it was a man's natural inclination to kill an uncle, because he does not want to admit that it might be his duty to kill him. He is really driven to talking as if some dark and secretive monomania alone prevented us all from killing our uncles. He is driven to this because he will not even take seriously the simple and, if you will, primitive morality upon which the tragedy is built. For that morality involves three moral propositions, from which the whole of the morbid modern subconsciousness does really recoil as from an ugly jar of pain. These principles are: first, that it may be our main business to do the right thing, even when we detest doing it; second, that the right thing may involve punishing some person, especially some powerful person; third, that the just process of punishment may take the form of fighting and killing. The modern critic is prejudiced against the first principle and calls it asceticism; he is prejudiced against the second principle and calls it

　　　　　　　　　　G. K. CHESTERTON

vindictiveness; he is prejudiced against the third and generally calls it militarism. That it actually might be the duty of a young man to risk his own life, much against his own inclination, by drawing a sword and killing a tyrant, that is an idea instinctively avoided by this particular mood of modern times. That is why tyrants have such a good time in modern times. And in order to avoid this plain and obvious meaning, of war as a duty and peace as a temptation, the critic has to turn the whole play upside down, and seek its meaning in modern notions so remote as to be in this connexion meaningless. He has to make William Shakespeare of Stratford one of the pupils of Professor Freud. He has to make him a champion of psycho-analysis, which is like making him a champion of vaccination. He has to fit Hamlet's soul somehow into the classifications of Freud and Jung; which is just as if he had to fit Hamlet's father into the classifications of Sir Oliver Lodge and Sir Arthur Conan Doyle. He has to interpret the whole thing by a new morality that Shakespeare had never heard of, because he has an intense internal dislike of the old morality that Shakespeare could not help hearing of. And that morality, which some of us believe to be based on a much more realistic psychology, is that punishment as punishment is a perfectly healthy process, not merely because it is reform, but also because it is expiation. What the modern world means by proposing to substitute pity for punishment is really very simple. It is that the modern world dare not punish those who are punishable, but only those who are pitiable. It would never touch anyone so important as King Claudius—or Kaiser William.

Now this truth is highly topical just now. The point about Hamlet was that he wavered, very excusably, in something that had to be done; and this is the point quite apart from whether we ourselves would have done it. That was pointed out long ago by Browning in "The Statue and the Bust." He argued that even if the motive for acting was bad, the motive for not acting was worse. And an action or inaction is judged by its real motive, not by whether somebody else might have done the same thing from a better motive. Whether or no the tyrannicide of Hamlet was a duty, it was accepted as a duty and it was shirked as a duty. And that is precisely true of a tyrannicide like that for which everybody clamoured at the conclusion of the Great War. It may have been right or wrong to punish the Kaiser; it was certainly even more right to punish the German generals and admirals for their atrocities. But even if it was wrong, it was not abandoned because it was wrong. It was abandoned because it was troublesome. It was abandoned for all those motives of weakness and mutability of mood which we associate with the name of Hamlet. It might be glory or ignominy to shed the blood of imperial enemies, but it is certainly ignominy to shout for what you dare not shed; "to fall a-cursing like a common drab, a scullion." Granted that we had no better motives than we had then or have now, it

G. K. CHESTERTON

would certainly have been more dignified if we had fatted all the region-kites with this slave's offal. The motive is the only moral test. A saint might provide us with a higher motive for forgiving the War-Lords who butchered Fryatt and Edith Cavell. But we have not forgiven the War-Lords. We have simply forgotten the War. We have not pardoned like Christ; we have only procrastinated like Hamlet. Our highest motive has been laziness; our commonest motive has been money. In this respect indeed I must apologize to the charming and chivalrous Prince of Denmark for comparing him, even on a single point, with the princes of finance and the professional politicians of our time. At least Hamlet did not spare Claudius solely because he hoped to get money out of him for the salaries of the Players, or meant to do a deal with him about wine supplied to Elsinore or debts contracted at Wittenburg. Still less was Hamlet acting entirely in the interests of Shylock, an inhabitant of the distant city of Venice. Doubtless Hamlet was sent to England in order that he might develop further these higher motives for peace and pardon. "'Twill not be noticed in him there; there the men are as mad as he."

It is therefore very natural that men should be trying to dissolve the moral problem of Hamlet into the unmoral elements of consciousness and unconsciousness. The sort of duty that Hamlet shirked is exactly the sort of duty that we are all shirking; that of dethroning injustice and vindicating truth. Many are now in a mood to deny that it is a duty because it is a danger. This applies, of course, not only to international but internal and especially industrial matters. Capitalism was allowed to grow into a towering tyranny in England because the English were always putting off their popular revolution, just as the Prince of Denmark put off his palace revolution. They lectured the French about their love of bloody revolutions, exactly as they are now lecturing the French about their love of bloody wars. But the patience which suffered England to be turned into a plutocracy was not the patience of the saints; it was that patience which paralysed the noble prince of the tragedy; *accidia* and the great refusal. In any case, the vital point is that by refusing to punish the powerful we soon lost the very idea of punishment; and turned our police into a mere persecution of the poor.

THE MEANING OF MOCK TURKEY

Having lately taken part in a pageant of Nursery Rhymes, in the character of Old King Cole, I meditated not so much on the glorious past of the great kingdom of Colchester, as on the more doubtful future of Nursery Rhymes. The Modern Movements cannot produce a nursery rhyme; it is one of the many such things they cannot even be conceived as doing. But if they cannot create the nursery rhyme, will they destroy it? The new poets have already abolished rhyme; and presumably the new educationalists will soon abolish nurseries. Or if they do not destroy, will they reform; which is worse? Nursery rhymes are a positive network of notions and allusions of which the enlightened disapprove. To take only my own allotted rhyme as an example, some might think the very mention of a king a piece of reactionary royalism, inconsistent with that democratic self-determination we all enjoy under some five Controllers and a committee of the Cabinet. Perhaps in the amended version he will be called President Cole. Probably he will be confused with Mr. G. D. H. Cole, the first President of the Guild Socialistic Republic. With the greatest admiration for Mr. Cole, I cannot quite picture him as so festive a figure; and I incline to think that the same influences will probably eliminate the festivity. It is said that America, having already abolished the bowl, is now attempting to abolish the pipe. After that it might very reasonably go on to abolish the fiddlers; for music can be far more maddening than wine. Tolstoy, the only consistent prophet of the Simple Life, did really go on to denounce music as a mere drug. Anyhow, it is quite intolerable that the innocent minds of children should be poisoned with the idea of anybody calling for his pipe and his bowl. There will have to be some other version, such as: "He called for his milk and he called for his lozenge," or whatever form of bodily pleasure is still permitted to mankind. This particular verse will evidently have to be altered a great deal; it is founded on so antiquated a philosophy, that I fear even the alteration will not be easy or complete. I am not sure, for instance, that there is not a memory of animism and spiritism in the very word "soul," used in calling the monarch a merry old soul. It would seem that some other simple phrase, such as "a merry old organism," might be used with advantage. Indeed it would have more advantages than one; for if the reader will say the amended line in a flowing and lyrical manner, he cannot but observe that the experiment has burst the fetters of formal metre, and achieved one of these larger and lovelier melodies that we associate with *vers libre*.

It is needless to note the numberless other examples of nursery rhymes to which the same criticism applies. Some of the other cases are even more shocking to the true scientific spirit. For instance,

G. K. CHESTERTON

in the typically old-world rhyme of "Girls and boys come out to play," there appear the truly appalling words: "Leave your supper and leave your sleep." As the great medical reformer of our day observed, in a striking and immortal phrase, "All Eugenists are agreed upon the importance of sleep." The case of supper may be more complex and controversial. If the supper were a really hygienic and wholesome supper, it might not be so difficult to leave it. But it is obvious that the whole vision which the rhyme calls up is utterly imcompatible with a wise educational supervision. It is a wild vision of children playing in the streets by moonlight, for all the world as if they were fairies. Moonlight, like music, is credited with a power of upsetting the reason; and it is at least obvious that the indulgence is both unseasonable and unreasonable. No scientific reformer desires hasty and destructive action; for his reform is founded on that evolution which has produced the anthropoid from the amoeba, a process which none have ever stigmatized as hasty. But when the eugenist recalls the reckless and romantic love affairs encouraged by such moonlight, he will have to consider seriously the problem of abolishing the moon.

But indeed I have much more sympathy with the simplicity of the baby who cries for the moon than with the sort of simplicity that dismisses the moon as all moonshine. And in truth I think that these two antagonistic types of simplicity are perhaps the pivotal terms of the present transition. It is a new thing called the Simple Life against an older thing which may be called the Simple Soul; possibly exemplified, so far as nursery rhymes are concerned, by the incident of Simple Simon. I prefer the old Simple Simon, who, though ignorant of the economic theory of exchange, had at least a positive and poetic enthusiasm for pies. I think him far wiser than the new Simple Simon, who simplifies his existence by means of a perverse and pedantic antipathy to pies. It is unnecessary to add that this philosophy of pies is applicable with peculiar force to mince-pies; and thus to the whole of the Christmas tradition which descended from the first carols to the imaginative world of Dickens. The morality of that tradition is much too simple and obvious to be understood to-day. Awful as it may seem to many modern people, it means no less than that Simple Simon should have his pies, even in the absence of his pennies.

But the philosophy of the two Simple Simons is plain enough. The former is an expansion of simplicity towards complexity; Simon, conscious that he cannot himself make pies, approaches them with an ardour not unmixed with awe. But the latter is a reaction of complexity towards simplicity; in other words, the other Simon refuses pies for various reasons, often including the fact that he has eaten too many of them. Most of the Simple Life as we see it to-day is, of course, a thing having this character of the surfeit or satiety of Simon, when he has become less simple and certainly less greedy. This reaction may take two diverse forms; it may send Simon searching for more and more expensive and extravagant confectionery, or it may reduce him to nibbling at some new kind of nut biscuit. For it may be noted, in passing, that it probably will not reduce him to eating dry bread. The Simple Life never accepts anything that is simple in the sense of self-evident and familiar. The thing must be uncommonly simple; it must not be simply common. Its philosophy must be something higher than the ordinary breakfast table, and something drier than dry bread. The usual process, as I have observed it in vegetarian and other summaries, seems in one sense indeed to be simple enough. The pie-man produces what looks like the same sort of pie, or is supposed to look like it; only it has thinner crust outside and nothing at all inside. Then instead of asking Simple Simon for a penny he asks him for a pound, or possibly a guinea or a five-pound note. And what is strangest of all, the customer is often so singularly Simple a Simon that he pays for it. For that is perhaps the final and most marked difference between Simon of the Simple Spirit and Simon of the Simple Life. It is the fact that the ardent and appreciative Simon was not in possession of a penny. The more refined and exalted Simon is generally in possession of far too many pennies. He is often very rich and needs to be; for the drier and thinner and emptier are the pies, the more he is charged for them. But this alone will reveal another side of the same paradox; and if it be possible to spend a lot of money on the Simple Life, it is also possible to make a great deal of money out of it. There are several self-advertisers doing very well out of the new self-denial. But wealth is always at one end of it or the other; and that is the great difference between the two Simons. Perhaps it is the difference between Simon Peter and Simon Magus.

I have before me a little pamphlet in which the most precise directions are given for a Mock Turkey, for a vegetarian mince-pie, and for a cautious and hygienic Christmas pudding. I have never quite understood why it should be a part of the Simple Life to have anything so deceptive and almost conspiratorial as an imitation turkey. The coarse and comic alderman may be expected, in his festive ribaldry, to mock a turtle; but surely a lean and earnest humanitarian ought not to mock a turkey. Nor do I understand the theory of the imitation in its relation to the ideal. Surely one who thinks meat-eating mere cannibalism ought not to arrange vegetables so as to look like an animal. It is as if a converted cannibal in the Sandwich Islands were to arrange joints of meat in the shape of a missionary. The missionaries would surely regard the proceedings of their convert with something less than approval, and perhaps with something akin to alarm. But the consistency of these concessions I will leave on one side, because I am not here concerned with the concessions but with the creed itself. And I am concerned with the creed not merely as affecting its practice in diet or cookery but its general theory. For the compilers of the little

G. K. CHESTERTON

book before me are great on philosophy and ethics. There are whole pages about brotherhood and fellowship and happiness and healing. In short, as the writer observes, we have "also some Mental Helps, as set forth in the flood of Psychology Literature to-day—but raised to a higher plane." It may be a little risky to set a thing forth in a flood, or a little difficult to raise a flood to a higher plane; but there is behind these rather vague expressions a very real modern intelligence and point of view, common to considerable numbers of cultivated people, and well worthy of some further study.

Under the title of "How to Think" there are twenty-four rules of which the first few are: "Empty Your Mind," "Think of the Best Things," "Appreciate," "Analyse," "Prepare Physically," "Prepare Mentally," and so on. I have met some earnest students of this school, who had apparently entered on this course, but at the time of our meeting had only graduated so far as the fulfilment of the first rule. It was more obvious, on the whole, that they had succeeded in the preliminary process of emptying the mind than that they had as yet thought of the best things, or analysed or appreciated anything in particular. But there were others, I willingly admit, who had really thought of certain things in a genuinely thoughtful fashion, though whether they were really the best things might involve a difference of opinion between us. Still, so far as they are concerned, it is a school of thought, and therefore worth thinking about.

Having been able to this extent to appreciate, I will now attempt to analyse. I have attempted to discover in my own mind where the difference between us really lies, apart from all these superficial jests and journalistic points; to ask myself why it is exactly that their ideal vegetarian differs so much from my ideal Christian. And the result of the concentrated contemplation of their ideal is, I confess, a somewhat impatient forward plunge in the progress of my initiation. I am strongly disposed to "Prepare Physically" for a conflict with the ideal vegetarian, with the holy hope of hitting him on the nose. In one of Mr. P. G. Wodehouse's stories the vegetarian rebukes his enemy for threatening to skin him, by reminding him that man should only think beautiful thoughts; to which the enemy gives the unanswerable answer: "Skinning you is a beautiful thought." In the same way I am quite prepared to think of the best things; but I think hitting the ideal vegetarian on the nose would be one of the best things in the world. This may be an extreme example; but it involves a much more serious principle. What such philosophers often forget is that among the best things in the world are the very things which their placid universalism forbids; and that there is nothing better or more beautiful than a noble hatred. I do not profess to feel it for them; but they themselves do not seem to feel it for anything.

But as my new idealistic instructor tells me to analyse, I will attempt to analyse. In the ordinary way it

G. K. CHESTERTON

would perhaps be enough to say that I do not like his ideals, and that I prefer my own, as I should say I did not like the taste of nut cutlet so much as the taste of veal cutlet. But just as it is possible to resolve the food into formulæ about proteids, so it is partly possible to resolve the religious preference into formulæ about principles. The most we can hope to do is to find out which of these principles are the first principles. And in this connexion I should like to speak a little more seriously, and even a little more respectfully, of the formula about emptying the mind. I do not deny that it is sometimes a good thing to empty the mind of the mere accumulation of secondary and tertiary impressions. If what is meant is something which a friend of mine once called "a mental spring clean," then I can see what it means. But the most drastic spring clean in a house does not generally wash away the house. It does not tear down the roof like a cobweb, or pluck up the walls like weeds. And the true formula is not so much to empty the mind as to discover that we cannot empty the mind, by emptying it as much as we can. In other words, we always come back to certain fundamentals which are convictions, because we can hardly even conceive their contraries. But it is the paradox of human language that though these truths are, in a manner past all parallel, hard and clear, yet any attempt to talk about them always has the appearance of being hazy and elusive.

Now this antagonism, when thus analysed, seems to me to arise from one ultimate thing at the back of the minds of these men; that they believe in taking the body seriously. The body is a sort of pagan god, though the pagans are more often stoics than epicureans. To begin with, it is itself a beginning. The body, if not the creator of the soul in heaven, is regarded as the practical producer of it on earth. In this their materialism is the very foundation of their asceticism. They wish us to consume clean fruit and clear water that our minds may be clear or our lives clean. The body is a sort of magical factory where these things go in as vegetables and come out as virtues. Thus digestion has the first sign of a deity; that of being an origin. It has the next sign of a deity; that if it is satisfied other things do not matter, or at any rate other things follow in their place. And so, they would say, the services of the body should be serious and not grotesque; and its smallest hints should be taken as terrible warnings. Art has a place in it because the body must be draped like an altar; and science is paraded in it because the service must be in Latin or Greek or something hieratic tongue. I quite understand these things surrounding a god or an altar; but I do not happen to worship at that altar or to believe in that god. I do not think the body ought to be taken seriously; I think it is far safer and saner when it is taken comically and even coarsely. And I think that when the body is given a holiday, as it is in a great feast, I think it should be set free not merely for wisdom but for folly, not merely to dance but to turn head over heels. In short, when it is really

G. K. CHESTERTON

allowed to exaggerate its own pleasures, it ought also to exaggerate its own absurdity. The body has its own rank, and its own rights, and its own place under government; but the body is not the King but rather the Court Jester. And the human and historical importance of the old jests and buffooneries of Christmas, however vulgar or stale or trivial they appear, is that in them the popular instinct always resisted this pagan solemnity about sensual things. A man was meant to feel rather a goose when he was eating goose; and to realize that he is such stuff as stuffing is made of. That is why anyone who has in these things the touch of the comic will also have the taste for the conservative; he will be unwilling to alter what that popular instinct has made in its own absurd image. He will be doubtful about a Christmas pudding moulded in the shape of the Pyramid or the Parthenon, or anything that is not as round and ridiculous as the world. And when Mr. Pickwick, as round and ridiculous as any Christmas pudding or any world worth living in, stood straddling and smiling under the mistletoe, he disinfected that vegetable of its ancient and almost vegetarian sadness and heathenism, of the blood of Baldur and the human sacrifice of the Druids.

SHAKESPEARE AND
THE LEGAL LADY

I wonder how long liberated woman will endure the invidious ban which excludes her from being a hangman. Or rather, to speak with more exactitude, a hangwoman. The very fact that there seems something vaguely unfamiliar and awkward about the word, is but a proof of the ages of sex oppression that have accustomed us to this sex privilege. The ambition would not perhaps have been understood by the prudish and sentimental heroines of Fanny Burney and Jane Austen. But it is now agreed that the farther we go beyond these faded proprieties the better; and I really do not see how we could go farther. There are always torturers of course; who will probably return under some scientific name. Obscurantists may use the old argument, that woman has never risen to the first rank in this or other arts; that Jack Ketch was not Jemima Ketch, and that the headsman was called Samson and not Delilah. And they will be overwhelmed with the old retort: that until we have hundreds of healthy women happily engaged in this healthful occupation, it will be impossible to judge whether they can rise above the average or no. Tearful sentimentalists may feel something unpleasing, something faintly repugnant, about the new feminine trade. But, as the indignant policewoman said the other day, when a magistrate excluded some of her sex and service from revolting revelations, "crime is a disease," and must be studied scientifically, however hideous it may be. Death also is a disease; and frequently a fatal one. Experiments must be made in it; and it must be inflicted in any form, however hideous, in a cool and scientific manner.

It is not true, of course, that crime is a disease. It is criminology that is a disease. But the suggestion about the painful duties of a policewoman leads naturally to my deduction about the painful duties of a hangwoman. And I make it in the faint hope of waking up some of the feminists, that they may at least be moved to wonder what they are doing, and to attempt to find out. What they are not doing is obvious enough. They are not asking themselves two perfectly plain questions; first, whether they want anybody to be a hangman; and second, whether they want everybody to be a hangman. They simply assume, with panting impetuosity, that we want everybody to be everything, criminologists, constables, barristers, executioners, torturers. It never seems to occur to them that some of us doubt the beauty and blessedness of these things, and are rather glad to limit them like other necessary evils. And this applies especially to the doubtful though defensible case of the advocate.

There is one phrase perpetually repeated and now practically stereotyped, which to my mind concentrates and sums up all the very worst qualities in the very worst journalism; all its paralysis of thought, all its monotony of chatter, all its sham culture and shoddy picturesqueness, all its perpetual readiness to cover any vulgarity of the present with any sentimentalism about the past. There is one phrase that does measure to how low an ebb the mind of my unfortunate profession can sink. It is the habit of perpetually calling any of the new lady barristers "Portia."

First of all, of course, it is quite clear that the journalist does not know who Portia was. If he has ever heard of the story of the "Merchant of Venice," he has managed to miss the only point of the story. Suppose a man had been so instructed in the story of "As You Like It" that he remained under the impression that Rosalind really was a boy, and was the brother of Celia. We should say that the plot of the comedy had reached his mind in a rather confused form. Suppose a man had seen a whole performance of the play of "Twelfth Night" without discovering the fact that the page called Cesario was really a girl called Viola. We should say that he had succeeded in seeing the play without exactly seeing the point. But there is exactly the same blind stupidity in calling a barrister Portia; or even in calling Portia a barrister. It misses in exactly the same sense the whole meaning of the scene. Portia is no more a barrister than Rosalind is a boy. She is no more the learned jurist whom Shylock congratulates than Viola is the adventurous page whom Olivia loves. The whole point of her position is that she is a heroic and magnanimous fraud. She has not taken up the legal profession, or any profession; she has not sought that public duty, or any public duty. Her action, from first to last, is wholly and entirely private. Her motives are not professional but private. Her ideal is not public but private. She acts as much on personal grounds in the Trial Scene as she does in the Casket Scene. She acts in order to save a friend, and especially a friend of the husband whom she loves. Anything less like the attitude of an advocate, for good or evil, could not be conceived. She seeks individually to save an individual; and in order to do so is ready to *break* all the existing laws of the profession and the public tribunal; to assume lawlessly powers she has not got, to intrude where she would never be legally admitted, to pretend to be somebody else, to dress up as a man; to do what is actually a crime against the law. This is not what is now called the attitude of a public woman; it is certainly not the attitude of a lady lawyer, any more than of any other kind of lawyer. But it is emphatically the attitude of a private woman; that much more ancient and much more powerful thing.

Suppose that Portia had really become an advocate, merely by advocating the cause of Antonio against Shylock. The first thing that follows is that, as like as not, she would be briefed in the next case to advocate the cause of Shylock against Antonio. She would, in the ordinary way of business, have to help Shylock to punish with ruin the private extravagances of Gratiano. She would have to assist Shylock to distrain on poor Launcelot Gobbo and sell up all his

G. K. CHESTERTON

miserable sticks. She might well be employed by him to ruin the happiness of Lorenzo and Jessica, by urging some obsolete parental power or some technical flaw in the marriage service. Shylock evidently had a great admiration for her forensic talents; and indeed that sort of lucid and detached admission of the talents of a successful opponent is a very Jewish characteristic. There seems no reason why he should not have employed her regularly, whenever he wanted some one to recover ruthless interest, to ruin needy households, to drive towards theft or suicide the souls of desperate men. But there seems every reason to doubt whether the Portia whom Shakespeare describes for us is likely to have taken on the job.

Anyhow, that is the job; and I am not here arguing that it is not a necessary job; or that it is always an indefensible job. Many honourable men have made an arguable case for the advocate who has to support Shylock, and men much worse than Shylock. But that is the job; and to cover up its ugly realities with a loose literary quotation that really refers to the exact opposite, is one of those crawling and cowardly evasions and verbal fictions which make all this sort of servile journalism so useless for every worthy or working purpose. If we wish to consider whether a lady should be a barrister, we should consider sanely and clearly what a barrister is and what a lady is; and then come to our conclusion according to what we consider worthy or worthless in the traditions of the two things. But the spirit of advertisement, which tries to associate soap with sunlight or grape-nuts with grapes, calls to its rescue an old romance of Venice and tries to cover up a practical problem in the robes of a romantic heroine of the stage. This is the sort of confusion that really leads to corruption. In one sense it would matter very little that the legal profession was formally open to women, for it is only a very exceptional sort of woman who would see herself as a vision of beauty in the character of Mr. Sergeant Buzfuz. And most girls are more likely to be stage-struck, and want to be the real Portia on the stage, rather than law-struck and want to be the very reverse of Portia in a law court. For that matter, it would make relatively little difference if formal permission were given to a woman to be a hangman or a torturer. Very few women would have a taste for it; and very few men would have a taste for the women who had a taste for it. But advertisement, by its use of the vulgar picturesque, can hide the realities of this professional problem, as it can hide the realities of tinned meats and patent medicines. It can conceal the fact that the hangman exists to hang, and that the torturer exists to torture. Similarly it can conceal the fact that the Buzfuz barrister exists to bully. It can hide from the innocent female aspirants outside even the perils and potential abuses that would be admitted by the honest male advocate inside. And that is part of a very much larger problem, which extends beyond this particular profession to a great many other professions; and not least to the lowest

G. K. CHESTERTON

and most lucrative of all modern professions; that of professional politics.

I wonder how many people are still duped by the story of the extension of the franchise. I wonder how many Radicals have been a little mystified, in remarking how many Tories and reactionaries have helped in the extension of the franchise. The truth is that calling in crowds of new voters will very often be to the interest, not only of Tories, but of really tyrannical Tories. It will often be in the interest of the guilty to appeal to the innocent; if they are innocent in the matter of other people's conduct as well as of their own. The tyrant calls in those he has not wronged, to defend him against those he has wronged. He is not afraid of the new and ignorant masses who know too little; he is afraid of the older and nearer nucleus of those who know too much. And there is nothing that would please the professional politician more than to flood the constituencies with innocent negroes or remote Chinamen, who might possibly admire him more, because they knew him less. I should not wonder if the Party System had been saved three or four times at the point of extinction, by the introduction of new voters who had never had time to discover why it deserved to be extinguished. The last of these rescues by an inrush of dupes was the enfranchisement of women.

What is true of the political is equally true of the professional ambition. Much of the mere imitation of masculine tricks and trades is indeed trivial enough;

it is a mere masquerade. The greatest of Roman satirists noted that in his day the more fast of the fashionable ladies liked to fight as gladiators in the amphitheatre. In that one statement he pinned and killed, like moths on a cork, a host of women prophets and women pioneers and large-minded liberators of their sex in modern England and America. But besides these more showy she-gladiators there are also multitudes of worthy and sincere women who take the new (or rather old) professions seriously. The only disadvantage is that in many of those professions they can only continue to be serious by ceasing to be sincere. But the simplicity with which they first set out is an enormous support to old and complex and corrupt institutions. No modest person setting out to learn an elaborate science can be expected to start with the assumption that it is not worth learning. The young lady will naturally begin to learn Law as gravely as she begins to learn Greek. It is not in that mood that she will conceive independent doubts about the ultimate relations of Law and Justice. Just as the Suffragettes are already complaining that the realism of industrial revolution interferes with their new hobby of voting, so the lady lawyers are quite likely to complain that the realism of legal reformers interferes with their new hobby of legalism. We are suffering in every department from the same cross-purposes that can be seen in the case of any vulgar patent medicine. In Law and Medicine, we have the thing advertised in the public press instead of analysed by the public

G. K. CHESTERTON

authority. What we want is not the journalistic Portia but the theatrical Portia; who is also the real Portia. We do not want the woman who will enter the law court with the solemn sense of a lasting vocation. We want a Portia; a woman who will enter it as lightly, and leave it as gladly as she did.

The same thing is true of a fact nobler than any fiction; the story, so often quoted, of the woman who won back mediæval France. Joan of Arc was a soldier; but she was not a normal soldier. If she had been, she would have been vowed, not to the war for France, but to any war with Flanders, Spain or the Italian cities to which her feudal lord might lead her. If she were a modern conscript, she would be bound to obey orders not always coming from St. Michael. But the point is here that merely making all women soldiers, under either system, could do nothing at all except whitewash and ratify feudalism or conscription. And both feudalism and conscription are much more magnanimous things than our modern system of police and prisons.

In fact there are few sillier implications than that in the phrase that what is sauce for the goose is sauce for the gander. A cook who really rules a kitchen on that principle would wait patiently for milk from the bull, because he got it from the cow. It is neither a perceptible fact nor a first principle that the sexes must not specialize; and if one sex must specialize in adopting dubious occupations, we ought to be very glad that the other sex specializes in abstaining from them. That is how the balance of criticism in the commonwealth is maintained; as by a sort of government and opposition. In this, as in other things, the new regime is that everybody shall join the government. The government of the moment will be monstrously strengthened; for everybody will be a tyrant and everybody will be a slave. The detached criticism of official fashions will disappear; and none was ever so detached as the deadly criticism that came from women. When all women wear uniforms, all women will wear gags; for a gag is part of every uniform in the world.

G. K. CHESTERTON

ON BEING AN OLD BEAN

I was looking at some press cuttings that had pursued me down to a remote cottage beside a river of Norfolk; and as it happened, those that caught my eye were mostly not from the vulgar monopolist press, but from all sorts of quieter and even more studious publications. But what struck me as curious about the collection as a whole was the selection, among half a hundred things that were hardly worth saying, of the things that were considered worth repeating. There seemed to be a most disproportionate importance attached to a trivial phrase I had used about the alleged indecorum of a gentleman calling his father an old bean. I had been asked to join in a discussion in the "Morning Post," touching the alleged disrespect of youth towards age, and I had done so; chiefly because I have a respect for the "Morning Post" for its courage about political corruption and cosmopolitan conspiracies, in spite of deep disagreement on other very vital things. And I said what I should have thought was so true as to be trite. I said that it makes life narrower and not broader to lose the special note of piety or respect for the past still living; and that to call an old man an old bean is merely to lose all intelligent sense of the significance of an old man. Since then, to my great entertainment, I seem to have figured in various papers as a sort of ferocious heavy father, come out on my own account to curse the numerous young sprigs who have called me an old bean. But this is an error. I should be the last to deny that I am heavy, but I am not fatherly; nor am I ferocious, at any rate I am not ferocious about this. Individually I regard the question with a detachment verging on indifference. I cannot imagine anybody except an aged and very lean vegetarian positively dancing with joy at being called an old bean; and I am not a very lean vegetarian. But still less can I imagine anyone regarding the accusation with horror or resentment; the sins and crimes blackening the career of a bean must be comparatively few; its character must be simple and free from complexity, and its manner of life innocent. A philosophic rationalist wrote to me the other day to say that my grubbing in the grossest superstitions of the past reminded him of "an old sow pig rooting in the refuse of the kitchen heap," and expressed a hope that I should be dragged from this occupation and made to resume "the cap and bells of yore." That is something like a vigorous and vivid comparison; though my Feminist friends may be distressed at my being compared to a sow as well as a pig; and though I am not quite clear myself about how the animal would get on when he had resumed the cap and bells of yore. But it would certainly be a pity, when it was possible to find this image in the kitchen heap, to be content with one from the kitchen garden. It would indeed be a lost opportunity to work yourself up to

G. K. CHESTERTON

the furious pitch of calling your enemy a beast, and then only call him a bean.

From the extracts I saw, it would seem that certain ladies wereespecially lively in their protest against my antiquated prejudices; and rioted in quite a bean-feast of old beans. The form the argument generally takes is to ask why parents and children should not be friends, or as they often put it (I deeply regret to say) pals. Neither term seems to me to convey a sufficiently distinctive meaning; and I take it that the best term for what they really mean is that they should be comrades. Now comradeship is a very real and splendid thing; but this is simply the cant of comradeship. A boy does not take his mother with him when he goes bird-nesting; and his affection for his mother is of another kind unconnected with the idea of her climbing a tree. Three men do not generally take an aged and beloved aunt with them as part of their luggage on a walking tour; and if they did, it would not be so much disrespectful to age as unjust to youth. For this confusion between two valuable but varied things, like most of such modern confusions, is quite as liable to obscurantist as to mutinous abuse; and is as easy to turn into tyranny as into licence. If a boy's aunts are his comrades, why should he need any comrades except his aunts? If his father and mother are perfect and consummate pals, why should he fool away his time with more ignorant, immature and insufficient pals? As in a good many other modern things, the end of the old parental dignity would be the beginning of a new parental tyranny. I would rather the boy loved his father as his father than feared him as a Frankenstein giant of a superior and supercilious friend, armed in that unequal friendship with all the weapons of psychology and psycho-analysis. If he loves him as a father he loves him as an older man; and if we are to abolish all differences of tone towards those older than ourselves, we must presumably do the same to those younger than ourselves. All healthy people, for instance, feel an instinctive and almost impersonal affection for a baby. Is a baby a comrade? Is he to climb the tree and go on the walking tour; or are we on his account to abolish all trees and tours? Are the grandfather aged ninety, the son aged thirty, and the grandson aged three, all to set out together on their travels, with the same knapsacks and knicker-bockers? I have read somewhere that in one of the Ten or Twelve or Two Hundred Types of Filial Piety reverenced by the Chinese, one was an elderly sage and statesman, who dressed up as a child of four and danced before his yet more elderly parents, to delight them with the romantic illusion that they were still quite young. This in itself could not but attract remark; but this in itself I am prepared to defend. It was an exceptional and even extraordinary festivity, like the reversals of the Saturnalia; and I wish we could have seen some vigorous old gentleman like Lord Halsbury or the Archbishop of Canterbury performing a similar act of piety. But in the Utopia of

G. K. CHESTERTON

comradeship now commended to us, old and young are expected normally to think alike, feel alike and talk alike; and may therefore normally and permanently be supposed to dress alike. Whether the parents dress as children or the children as parents, it is clear that they must all dress as pals, whatever be the ceremonial dress of that rank. I imagine it as something in tweeds, with rather a loud check.

As I considered these things I looked across the kitchen garden of the cottage, and the association of peas and beans brought the fancy back to the foolish figure of speech with which the discussion began. There is a proverb, which is like most of our popular sayings, a country proverb, about things that are as like as two peas. There is something significant in the fact that this is as near as the rural imagination could get to a mere mechanical monotony. For as a matter of fact it is highly improbable that any two peas are exactly alike. A survey of the whole world of peas, with all their forms and uses, would probably reveal every sort of significance between the sweet peas of sentiment and the dried peas of asceticism. Modern machinery has gone far beyond such rude rural attempts at dullness. Things are not as like as two peas in the sense that they are as like as two pins. But the flippant phrase under discussion does really imply that they are as like as two beans. It is really part of the low and levelling philosophy that assimilates all things too much to each other. It does not mean that we see any fanciful significance in the use of the term, as in a country proverb. It is not that we see an old gentleman with fine curling white hair and say to him poetically, "Permit me, venerable cauliflower, to inquire after your health." It is not that we address an old farmer with a deep and rich complexion, saying, "I trust, most admirable of beet-roots, that you are as well as you look." When we say, "How are you, old bean," the error is not so much that we say something rude, but that we say nothing because we mean nothing.

As I happened to meet at that moment a girl belonging to the family of the cottage, I showed her the cutting, and asked her opinion upon the great progressive problem of calling your father an old bean. At which she laughed derisively, and merely said, "As if anybody would!"

G. K. CHESTERTON

THE FEAR OF THE FILM

Long lists are being given of particular cases in which children have suffered in spirits or health from alleged horrors of the kinema. One child is said to have had a fit after seeing a film; another to have been sleepless with some fixed idea taken from a film; another to have killed his father with a carving-knife through having seen a knife used in a film. This may possibly have occurred; though if it did, anybody of common sense would prefer to have details about that particular child, rather than about that particular picture. But what is supposed to be the practical moral of it, in any case? Is it that the young should never see a story with a knife in it? Are they to be brought up in complete ignorance of "The Merchant of Venice" because Shylock flourishes a knife for a highly disagreeable purpose? Are they never to hear of Macbeth, lest it should slowly dawn upon their trembling intelligence that it is a dagger that they see before them? It would be more practical to propose that a child should never see a real carving-knife, and still more practical that he should never see a real father. All that may come; the era of preventive and prophetic science has only begun. We must not be impatient. But when we come to the cases of morbid panic after some particular exhibition, there is yet more reason to clear the mind of cant. It is perfectly true that a child will have the horrors after seeing some particular detail. It is quite equally true that nobody can possibly predict what that detail will be. It certainly need not be anything so obvious as a murder or even a knife. I should have thought anybody who knew anything about children, or for that matter anybody who had been a child, would know that these nightmares are quite incalculable. The hint of horror may come by any chance in any connexion. If the kinema exhibited nothing but views of country vicarages or vegetarian restaurants, the ugly fancy is as likely to be stimulated by these things as by anything else. It is like seeing a face in the carpet; it makes no difference that it is the carpet at the vicarage.

I will give two examples from my own most personal circle; I could give hundreds from hearsay. I know a child who screamed steadily for hours if he had been taken past the Albert Memorial. This was not a precocious precision or excellence in his taste in architecture. Nor was it a premature protest against all that gimcrack German culture which nearly entangled us in the downfall of the barbaric tyranny. It was the fear of something which he himself described with lurid simplicity as The Cow with the India-rubber Tongue. It sounds rather a good title for a creepy short story. At the base of the Albert Memorial (I may explain for those who have never enjoyed that monument) are four groups of statuary representing Europe, Asia, Africa, and America.

G. K. CHESTERTON

America especially is very overwhelming; borne onward on a snorting bison who plunges forward in a fury of western progress, and is surrounded with Red Indians, Mexicans, and all sorts of pioneers, O pioneers, armed to the teeth. The child passed this transatlantic tornado with complete coolness and indifference. Europe however is seated on a bull so mild as to look like a cow; the tip of its tongue is showing and happened to be discoloured by weather; suggesting, I suppose, a living thing coming out of the dead marble. Now nobody could possibly foretell that a weather-stain would occur in that particular place, and fill that particular child with that particular fancy. Nobody is likely to propose meeting it by forbidding graven images, like the Moslems and the Jews. Nobody has said (as yet) that it is bad morals to make a picture of a cow. Nobody has even pleaded that it is bad manners for a cow to put its tongue out. These things are utterly beyond calculation; they are also beyond counting, for they occur all over the place, not only to morbid children but to any children. I knew this particular child very well, being a rather older child myself at the time. He certainly was not congenitally timid or feeble-minded; for he risked going to prison to expose the Marconi Scandal and died fighting in the Great War.

Here is another example out of scores. A little girl, now a very normal and cheerful young lady, had an insomnia of insane terror entirely arising from the lyric of "Little Bo-Peep." After an inquisition like that of the confessor or the psycho-analyst, it was found that the word "bleating" had some obscure connexion in her mind with the word "bleeding." There was thus perhaps an added horror in the phrase "heard"; in hearing rather than seeing the flowing of blood. Nobody could possibly provide against that sort of mistake. Nobody could prevent the little girl from hearing about sheep, any more than the little boy from hearing about cows. We might abolish all nursery rhymes; and as they are happy and popular and used with universal success, it is very likely that we shall. But the whole point of the mistake about that phrase is that it might have been a mistake about any phrase. We cannot foresee all the fancies that might arise, not only out of what we say, but of what we do not say. We cannot avoid promising a child a caramel lest he should think we say cannibal, or conceal the very word "hill" lest it should sound like "hell."

All the catalogues and calculations offered us by the party of caution in this controversy are therefore quite worthless. It is perfectly true that examples can be given of a child being frightened of this, that or the other. But we can never be certain of his being frightened of the same thing twice. It is not on the negative side, by making lists of vetoes, that the danger can be avoided; it can never indeed be entirely avoided. We can only fortify the child on the positive side by giving him health and humour and a trust in God; not omitting (what will much mystify the moderns) an intelligent appreciation of the idea of

G. K. CHESTERTON

authority, which is only the other side of confidence, and which alone can suddenly and summarily cast out such devils. But we may be sure that most modern people will not look at it in this way. They will think it more scientific to attempt to calculate the incalculable. So soon as they have realized that it is not so simple as it looks, they will try to map it out, however complicated it may be. When they discover that the terrible detail need not be a knife, but might just as well be a fork, they will only say there is a fork complex as well as a knife complex. And that increasing complexity of complexes is the net in which liberty will be taken.

Instead of seeing in the odd cases of the cow's tongue or the bleating sheep the peril of their past generalizations, they will see them only as starting points for new generalizations. They will get yet another theory out of it. And they will begin acting on the theory long before they have done thinking about it. They will start out with some new and crude conception that sculpture has made children scream or that nursery rhymes have made children sleepless; and the thing will be a clause in a programme of reform before it has begun to be a conclusion in a serious study of psychology. That is the practical problem about modern liberty which the critics will not see; of which eugenics is one example and all this amateur child-psychology is another. So long as an old morality was in black and white like a chessboard, even a man who wanted more of it made white was certain that no more of it would be made black. Now he is never certain what vices may not be released, but neither is he certain what virtues may be forbidden. Even if he did not think it wrong to run away with a married woman, he knew that his neighbours only thought it wrong because the woman was married. They did not think it wrong to run away with a red-haired woman, or a left-handed woman, or a woman subject to headaches. But when we let loose a thousand eugenical speculations, all adopted before they are verified and acted on even before they are adopted, he is just as likely as not to find himself separated from the woman for those or any other reasons. Similarly there was something to be said for restrictions, even rather puritanical and provincial restrictions, upon what children should read or see, so long as they fenced in certain fixed departments like sex or sensational tortures. But when we begin to speculate on whether other sensations may not stimulate as dangerously as sex, those other sensations may be as closely controlled as sex. When, let us say, we hear that the eye and brain are weakened by the rapid turning of wheels as well as by the most revolting torturing of men, we have come into a world in which cart-wheels and steam-engines may become as obscene as racks and thumbscrews. In short, so long as we *combine* ceaseless and often reckless scientific speculation with rapid and often random social reform, the result must inevitably be not anarchy but ever-increasing tyranny. There must

G. K. CHESTERTON

be a ceaseless and almost mechanical multiplication of things forbidden. The resolution to cure all the ills that flesh is heir to, combined with the guesswork about all possible ills that flesh and nerve and brain-cell may be heir to—these two things conducted simultaneously must inevitably spread a sort of panic of prohibition. Scientific imagination and social reform between them will quite logically and almost legitimately have made us slaves. This seems to me a very clear, a very fair and a very simple point of public criticism; and I am much mystified about why so many publicists cannot even see what it is, but take refuge in charges of anarchism, which firstly are not true, and secondly have nothing to do with it.

WINGS AND THE HOUSEMAID

Among the numberless fictitious things that I have fortunately never written, there was a little story about a logical maiden lady engaging apartments in which she was not allowed to keep a cat or dog, who, nevertheless, stipulated for permission to keep a bird, and who eventually walked round to her new lodgings accompanied by an ostrich. There was a moral to the fable, connected with that exaggeration of small concessions, in which, for instance, the Germans indulged about espionage, or the Jews about interest. But this faded fancy returned to my mind in another fashion when a very humane lady suggested the other day that every domestic servant, including the butler, I presume, should be described as "a home-bird." Unless the lady is mis-reported, which is likely enough, she wanted servants called home-birds because they keep the home-fires burning, which, as many will be ready to point out, is hardly the particular form in which the domesticity of the nest commonly expresses itself. But I am not at all disposed to deride the lady's real meaning, still less her real motives, which referred to a real movement of social conscience and sentiment, however wrongly expressed. She was troubled about the implied insolence of calling servants servants and apparently even of talking about "maids" or "the cook."

Therefore she evolved the ornithological substitute; about which, of course, it would be easy to evolve a whole aviary of allegorical parodies. It would be easy to ask whether a private secretary is to be called a secretary bird, or, perhaps, the telephone girl a humming-bird. But it will be enough to say generally of the proposal, in its present verbal form, that one has only to submit it to any living and human housemaid in order to find that particular home-bird developing rapidly into a mockingbird. Nevertheless, as I have said, we should not merely dismiss any social doubts thus suggested, or any impulse towards a warmer respect for work generally grossly undervalued. Too many people, of the more snobbish social strata, have treated their servants as home-birds; as owls, for instance, who can be up all night, or as vultures, who can eat the refuse fit for the dustbin. I would not throw cold water on any indignation on this score; but I note it as typical of the time that the indignation should fail on the side of intelligence. For it is the mark of our time, above almost everything else, that it goes by associations and not by arguments; that is why it has a hundred arts and no philosophy.

Thus, for instance, the lady in question lumps together a number of terms that have no logical connexion at all. There is at least a meaning in objecting to one person calling another a servant. As I shall suggest in a moment, there is not much sense in changing the name when you do not change the thing; and there is a great deal of nonsense in denying the status

G. K. CHESTERTON

of the servant at the moment when you are making it more servile. Still, anybody can see how the term might be held to hurt human dignity; but the other terms mentioned cannot hurt human dignity at all. I cannot conceive why it should insult a cook to call her a cook, any more than it insults a cashier to call him a cashier; to say nothing of the fact that dealing with cookery is far nobler than dealing with cash. And the third title certainly tells entirely the other way. The word "maid" is not only a noble old English word, with no note of social distinction; for a mediæval king might have praised his daughter as "a good maid." It is a word loaded with magnificent memories, in history, literature, and religion. Joan the Maid suggests a little more than Joan the maid-servant. As it says in Mr. Belloc's stirring little poem:—

By God who made the Master Maids,
I know not whence she came;
But the sword she bore to save the soul
Went up like an altar flame.

It is needless here to trace the idea back to its splendid sources; or to explain how the word maid has been the highest earthly title, not only on earth but in heaven. "Mother and maiden was never none but she." Here at least modern humanitarian criticism has gone curiously astray, even for its own purposes; any servant may well be satisfied with the dignity of being called the maid, just as any workman may be rightly honoured by the accident which calls him the man. For in a modern industrial dispute, as reported in the papers, I always feel there is a final verdict and sentence in the very statement of the case of Masters *versus* Men.

The true objection lies much farther back. It begins with the simple fact that the home-bird is not in her own home. When that particular sparrow stokes the fire, as above described, it is not her own fireside; when we happen to meet a canary carrying a coalscuttle, the canary is not generally a coal-owner. In short, wherever we find pelicans, penguins, or flamingoes keeping the home-fires burning, they may all be earnestly wishing that they could fly away to their homes. Now a moderate amount of this temporary and vicarious domesticity is a natural enough accident in social relations, so long as it does not obscure and obstruct more individual and direct domesticity. In short, there is no particular harm in the maid being a housemaid in someone else's house, if she normally has a chance of being a housewife in her own. As I shall suggest in a moment, this is what was really implied in certain older institutions to which the wisest are now looking back. But in any case it is odd that the home-bird should thus plume itself at this moment; for the trend of the time is certainly not towards any domesticity, direct or indirect. The birds have long been netted or caged, by cold, fear and hunger, into larger and more terrorist systems. The happy home-birds are keeping the

G. K. CHESTERTON

factory fires burning. The only legal and industrial tendency seems to be to shut up more and more of the women, those strange wild fowl, in those colossal cages of iron. Nor is the change one of mere æsthetic atmosphere; we know now that it is one of economic fact and may soon be one of legal definition. In a word, it is queer that we should suddenly grow sensitive about calling people servants when we are in the act of making them slaves. Indeed, in many concrete cases we may already be said to be making them convicts. The true moral meaning of much that is called the improvement of prisons is not that we are turning prisoners into a better sort of people, but rather that we are treating a better sort of people as prisoners. The broad arrow is broadened in so liberal a fashion as to cover those who would once have been counted respectable; and there is a sense in which the broad arrow, becoming broader, is bound to become blunter. The prison becomes utilitarian as well as disciplinary, as the factory becomes disciplinary as well as utilitarian. The two become simply and substantially the same; for they have to treat the same sort of impecunious people in the same sort of impersonal way. People may differ about the definition of that common condition or status. Some may eagerly salute persons involved as home-birds. Others may prefer to describe them as jail-birds.

For the rest, if anybody wants to strike the central stream of moderate sanity in the servant problem, I recommend him first to read with a close attention or preferably to sing in a loud voice, the song called "Sally in Our Alley." In that great and gloriously English lyric, the poet does not disguise the accidental discomforts of the great system of apprenticeship which was part of the glory of the Guilds. He even exhibits his Christian prejudices by comparing his master to a Turk. He actually entertains, as every reflective social reformer must, the hypothetical alternative of the Servile State, and considers the relative advantages of a slave that rows a galley. But the point is that what makes him refuse and endure is hope, the sure and certain hope of a glorious emancipation; not the hopeless hope of a chance in a scramble, with a general recommendation to get on or get out, but a charter of knowledge and honour, that "when his seven long years are past," a door shall open to him, which our age has shut on the great multitude of mankind.

THE SLAVERY OF FREE VERSE

The truth most needed to-day is that the end is never the right end. The beginning is the right end at which to begin. The modern man has to read everything backwards; as when he reads journalism first and history afterwards—if at all. He is like a blind man exploring an elephant, and condemned to begin at the very tip of its tail. But he is still more unlucky; for when he has a first principle, it is generally the very last principle that he ought to have. He starts, as it were, with one infallible dogma about the elephant; that its tail is its trunk. He works the wrong way round on principle; and tries to fit all the practical facts to his principle. Because the elephant has no eyes in its tail-end, he calls it a blind elephant; and expatiates on its ignorance, superstition, and need of compulsory education. Because it has no tusks at its tail-end, he says that tusks are a fantastic flourish attributed to a fabulous creature, an ivory chimera that must have come through the ivory gate. Because it does not as a rule pick up things with its tail, he dismisses the magical story that it can pick up things with its trunk. He probably says it is plainly a piece of anthropomorphism to suppose that an elephant can pack its trunk. The result is that he becomes as pallid and worried as a pessimist; the world to him is not only an elephant, but a white elephant. He does not know what to do with it, and cannot be persuaded of the perfectly simple explanation; which is that he has not made the smallest real attempt to make head or tail of the animal. He will not begin at the right end; because he happens to have come first on the wrong end.

But in nothing do I feel this modern trick, of trusting to a fag-end rather than a first principle, more than in the modern treatment of poetry. With this or that particular metrical form, or unmetrical form, or unmetrical formlessness, I might be content or not, as it achieved some particular effect or not. But the whole general tendency, regarded as an emancipation, seems to me more or less of an enslavement. It seems founded on one subconscious idea; that talk is freer than verse; and that verse, therefore, should claim the freedom of talk. But talk, especially in our time, is not free at all. It is tripped up by trivialities, tamed by conventions, loaded with dead words, thwarted by a thousand meaningless things. It does not liberate the soul so much, when a man can say, "You always look so nice," as when he can say, "But your eternal summer shall not fade." The first is an awkward and constrained sentence ending with the weakest word ever used, or rather misused, by man. The second is like the gesture of a giant or the sweeping flight of an archangel; it has the very rush of liberty. I do not despise the man who says the first, because he *means* the second; and what he means is more important than what he says. I have always

G. K. CHESTERTON

done my best to emphasize the inner dignity of these daily things, in spite of their dull externals; but I do not think it an improvement that the inner spirit itself should grow more external and more dull. It is thought right to discourage numbers of prosaic people trying to be poetical; but I think it much more of a bore to watch numbers of poetical people trying to be prosaic. In short, it is another case of tail-foremost philosophy; instead of watering the laurel hedge of the cockney villa, we bribe the cockney to brick in the plant of Apollo.

I have always had the fancy that if a man were really free, he would talk in rhythm and even in rhyme. His most hurried post-card would be a sonnet; and his most hasty wires like harp-strings. He would breathe a song into the telephone; a song which would be a lyric or an epic, according to the time involved in awaiting the call; or in his inevitable altercation with the telephone girl, the duel would be also a duet. He would express his preference among the dishes at dinner in short impromptu poems, combining the more mystical gratitude of grace with a certain epigrammatic terseness, more convenient for domestic good feeling. If Mr. Yeats can say, in exquisite verse, the exact number of bean-rows he would like on his plantation, why not the number of beans he would like on his plate? If he can issue a rhymed request to procure the honey-bee, why not to pass the honey? Misunderstandings might arise at first with the richer and more fantastic poets; and Francis Thompson might have asked several times for "the gold skins of undelirious wine" before anybody understood that he wanted the grapes. Nevertheless, I will maintain that his magnificent phrase would be a far more real expression of God's most glorious gift of the vine, than if he had simply said in a peremptory manner "grapes"; especially if the culture of compulsory education had carefully taught him to pronounce it as if it were "gripes." And if a man could ask for a potato in the form of a poem, the poem would not be merely a more romantic but a much more realistic rendering of a potato. For a potato is a poem; it is even an ascending scale of poems; beginning at the root, in subterranean grotesques in the Gothic manner, with humps like the deformities of a goblin and eyes like a beast of Revelation, and rising up through the green shades of the earth to a crown that has the shape of stars and the hue of heaven.

But the truth behind all this is that expressed in that very ancient mystical notion, the music of the spheres. It is the idea that, at the back of everything, existence begins with a harmony and not a chaos; and, therefore, when we really spread our wings and find a wider freedom, we find it in something more continuous and recurrent, and not in something more fragmentary and crude. Freedom is fullness, especially fullness of life; and a full vessel is more rounded and complete than an empty one, and not less so. To vary Browning's phrase, we find in prose the broken arcs, in poetry the perfect round. Prose

G. K. CHESTERTON

is not the freedom of poetry; rather prose is the fragments of poetry. Prose, at least in the prosaic sense, is poetry interrupted, held up and cut off from its course; the chariot of Phœbus stopped by a block in the Strand. But when it begins to move again at all, I think we shall find certain old-fashioned things move with it, such as repetition and even measure, rhythm and even rhyme. We shall discover with horror that the wheels of the chariot go round and round; and even that the horses of the chariot have the usual number of feet.

Anyhow, the right way to encourage the cortège is not to put the cart before the horse. It is not to make poetry more poetical by ignoring what distinguishes it from prose. There may be many new ways of making the chariot move again; but I confess that most of the modern theorists seem to me to be lecturing on a new theory of its mechanics, while it is standing still. If a wizard before my very eyes works a miracle with a rope, a boy and a mango plant, I am only theoretically interested in the question of a sceptic, who asks why it should not be done with a garden hose, a maiden aunt and a monkey-tree. Why not, indeed, if he can do it? If a saint performs a miracle to-morrow, by turning a stone into a fish, I shall be the less concerned at being asked, in the abstract, why a man should not also turn a camp-stool into a cockatoo; but let him do it, and not merely explain how it can be done. It is certain that words such as "birds" and "bare," which are as plain as "fish" or "stone," can be combined in such a miracle as "Bare ruined quires where late the sweet birds sang." So far as I can follow my own feelings, the metre and fall of the feet, even the rhyme and place in the sonnet, have a great deal to do with producing such an effect. I do not say there is no other way of producing such an effect. I only ask, not without longing, where else in this wide and weary time is it produced? I know I cannot produce it; and I do not in fact feel it when I hear *vers libres*. I know not where is that Promethean heat; and, even to express my ignorance, I am glad to find better words than my own.

G. K. CHESTERTON

PROHIBITION AND THE PRESS

An organ of the Nonconformist Conscience, while commenting very kindly on my recent remarks about America, naturally went on to criticize, though equally kind, my remarks about Prohibition. Now, so far as I am concerned, the problem is not so much Prohibition with a large P as prohibition with a small one. I mean, I am interested not so much in liquor as in liberty. I want to know on what principle the prohibitionists are proceeding in this case, and how they think it applies to any other case. And I cannot for the life of me make out. They might be expected to argue that there is something peculiar in principle about the position of liquor, and make that the basis for attacking liquor. But in point of fact they do not attack liquor; they do quite simply attack liberty. I mean that they are satisfied with saying about this liberty what can obviously be said about any liberty—that it can be, and is, abominably abused. If that had been a final objection to any form of freedom, there never would have been any form of freedom. And there most notably would never have been the particular forms of freedom which are most sacred to the Nonconformist Conscience. The Nonconformists have demanded liberty to secede, though they knew it led to an anarchy of sects and spiteful controversies. They have demanded the licence to print, though they knew it involved the licence to print twenty falsehoods to one truth. I suppose there is nothing in history of which the modern Puritan would be more innocently proud than the thing called the Liberty of the Press, which arose out of the pamphleteering of the seventeenth century, and especially the great pamphlet of Milton. Yet everything that Milton says, about allowing controversy in spite of its dangers, could be applied word for word to the case of allowing drinking in spite of its dangers. Is not the virtue that shuts itself up in a temperance hotel a fugitive and cloistered virtue? Is not the morality that dare not have wine on the table, or in the town, emphatically one that dares not sally out to meet its enemy? All Milton's arguments for freedom are arguments for beer; and, of course, Milton himself would certainly have applied them to beer. The highly successful brewer to whom he was Latin secretary—a gentleman of the name of Williams, otherwise Cromwell—would hardly have been pleased with him if he had not applied them to beer.

For instance, the critic whom I am here venturing to criticize says that people differ about Prohibition according to their knowledge or ignorance of the dreadful state of the slums, the ravages of alcoholism in our industrial cities, and all the rest of it. Whether or no this be a good argument against the public-house, there is no doubt that I could easily turn it against the public press. I could insist that I am a common Cockney Fleet Street journalist who has done nightly work for daily papers and fed off

G. K. CHESTERTON

nocturnal potato-stalls; whereas he is probably a culti-vated Congregationalist minister writing in a library of theological works. I might say that I know better than he does, or than most people do, the cynicism and the vulgarity and the vices of journalism. But, as a matter of fact, the vices of journalism have by this time become as evident to the people who read jour-nals as to the people who write them. All responsible people are complaining of the power and condition of the press, and no people more than these earnest and ethical Nonconformists. It is they who complain most bitterly that a Jingo press can manufacture war. It is they who declare most indignantly that a sen-sational press is undermining morality. They often, to my mind, unduly confuse matters of morality with matters of taste. They often, to my mind, denounce as mere Jingoism what is simply the deeply democratic and popular character of patriotism. But nobody will deny that to a large extent they are legitimately and logically alarmed about the abuses and absurdities of the newspapers. But they have not yet used this as an argument for a veto upon all newspapers. Why in the world should they use the parallel evils as an argument for a veto on all public-houses?

For my part I do feel very strongly about the frivol-ity and irresponsibility of the press. It seems impos-sible to exaggerate the evil that can be done by a cor-rupt and unscrupulous press. If drink directly ruins the family, it only indirectly ruins the nation. But bad journalism does directly ruin the nation, considered as a nation; it acts on the corporate national will and sways the common national decision. It may force a decision in a few hours that will be an incurable calamity for hundreds of years. It may drive a whole civilization to defeat, to slavery, to bankruptcy, to universal famine. Even at this moment there are prominent papers wildly urging us to war—not with our foes but with our friends. There are some journalists so wicked as to want war, almost for its own sake; there are more journalists so weak-minded as to work for war without even wanting it. Let me give one example out of fifty of the sort of phrases that flash by us when we turn over the papers. A headline in enormous letters announces that the French are "scuttling" out of the disputed areas in the Near East. The phrase about scuttling, and the policy of scuttle, has been familiar and firmly established in English journalism as meaning a cowardly and servile surrender, admitting abject defeat. And the suggestion is that the French, being notoriously a nation of cowards, having that tendency to panic produced by a habit of dancing and a diet of frogs, can vividly be pictured as scampering with screams of terror from the sight of a Turk with a drawn sabre. This is the way our newspapers improve our relations with our Allies. Only the newspaper men seem to have got a little mixed in their eagerness to expatiate on the wide field of French vileness and ignominy. Only a little while ago the same papers were telling us that the French were furious filibusters, forcing war in

G. K. CHESTERTON

every corner of the world. We were told that it was France which was militaristic and aggressive, and all her rivals were made to scuttle. We were told that it was the Frenchman and not the Turk who was the terrible person holding the drawn sabre. In plain words, these journalists are resolved to show that whatever the French do is wrong. If they advance, they are arrogant; if they retreat, they are cowardly. If they keep an army beyond the Rhine, they are pursuing a policy of militarism; if they withdraw an army from somewhere else, they are pursuing a policy of scuttle. Where M. Poincaré is ready to fight, he is a fire-eater who cares for nothing but fighting; where he is not ready to fight, he is a poltroon who is always notoriously too timid to fight. The careful selection of language of this sort, for a given period, might quite possibly land us in a European war—a war in which we should be certainly on the wrong side, and almost certainly on the losing side.

Suppose I come forward with this great reform of the Prohibition of the Press. Suppose I suggest that the police should forcibly shut up all the newspaper-offices, as the other reformers wish to shut up all the public-houses. What answer will the Puritan moralists make to me, or on what principle do they distinguish between the one reform and the other? There is no kind of doubt about the harm that journalism does; and their own line of argument precludes them from appealing merely to the good that it does. As a matter of fact, far better poems have been written in taverns than are ever likely to appear in daily papers. And, from Pantagruel to Pickwick, this form of festivity has a roll of literary glory to its credit which is never likely to be found in the back files of any newspaper that I know of. But the Puritans do not discuss the healthier tradition of wine; they consider their argument sufficiently supported by the unhealthy effects of gin and bad beer in the slums. And if we adopt that principle of judging by the worst, then the worst effects of the press are far wider than the worst effects of the public-house. What exactly is the principle by which they distinguish between lawful and unlawful liberty, or mixed and unmixed licence? I have a rough-and-ready test, which may be right or wrong, but which I can at least state; but where has their test been stated? I say that the simplest form of freedom is that which distinguishes the free man from the slave—the ownership of his own body and his own bodily activities. That there is a risk in allowing him this ownership is obvious, and has always been obvious. The risk is not confined to the question of drink, but covers the whole question of health. But surely the other forms of freedom, such as freedom to print, are very much more indirect and disputable. A newspaper may be made the instrument of the vilest sort of swindling or starving of a whole people. Why are we to grant the remote right, and deny the intimate right? Moreover, a newspaper is a new thing; if our fathers had the right to it, they never knew it. Fermented liquor

G. K. CHESTERTON

is as old as civilization, or older. But what I have asked for again and again is simply the principle of the Prohibitionists: and I am asking still.

THE MERCY OF
MR. ARNOLD BENNETT

Mr. Arnold Bennett recently wrote one of his humorous and humane *causeries*, pleading very properly for social imagination and the better understanding of our fellows. He carried it however to the point of affirming, as some fatalists do, that we should never judge anybody in the sense of condemning anybody, in connexion with his moral conduct. Some time ago the same distinguished writer showed that his mercy and magnanimity were indeed on a heroic scale by reviewing a book of mine, and even saying many kind things about it. But to these he added a doubt about whether true intelligence could be consistent with the acceptance of any dogma. In truth there are only two kinds of people; those who accept dogmas and know it, and those who accept dogmas and don't know it. My only advantage over the gifted novelist lies in my belonging to the former class. I suspect that his unconsciousness of his dogmas extends to an unconsciousness of what he means by a dogma. If it means merely the popular idea of being dogmatic, it might be suggested that saying that all dogmatism is unintelligent is itself somewhat dogmatic. And something of what is true of his veto on dogma is also true on his veto of condemnation; which is really a veto on vetoes.

Mr. Arnold Bennett does not darken the question with the dreary metaphysics of determinism; he is far too bright and adroit a journalist for that. But he does make a simple appeal to charity, and even Christianity, basing on it the idea that we should not judge people at all, or even blame them at all. Like everybody else who argues thus, he imagines himself to be pleading for mercy and humanity. Like everybody else who argues thus, he is doing the direct contrary. This particular notion of not judging people really means hanging them without trial. It would really substitute for judgment not mercy but something much more like murder. For the logical process through which the discussion passes is always the same; I have seen it in a hundred debates about fate and free-will. First somebody says, like Mr. Bennett: "Let us be kinder to our brethren, and not blame them for faults we cannot judge." Then some casual common-sense person says: "Do you really mean you would let anybody pick your pocket or cut your throat without protest?" Then the first man always answers as Mr. Bennett does: "Oh no; I would punish him to protect myself and protect society; but I would not *blame* him, because I would not venture to judge him." The philosopher seems to have forgotten that he set out with the idea of being kinder to the cut-throat and the pick-pocket. His sense of humour should suggest to him that the pick-pocket might possibly prefer to be blamed, rather than go to penal servitude for the protection of society.

Now of course Mr. Bennett is quite right in the most mystical and therefore the most deeply moral sense.

G. K. CHESTERTON

We do not know what God knows about the merits of a man. Nor do we know what God knows about the needs of a community. A man who poisons his little niece for money may have mysterious motives and excuses we cannot understand. And so he may serve mysterious social purposes we cannot follow. We are not infallible when we think we are punishing criminals; but neither are we infallible when we think we are protecting society. Our inevitable ignorance seems to me to cut both ways. But even in our ignorance one thing is vividly clear. Mr. Bennett's solution is not the more merciful, but the less merciful of the two. To say that we may punish people, but not blame them, is to say that we have a right to be cruel to them, but not a right to be kind to them.

For after all, blame is itself a compliment. It is a compliment because it is an appeal; and an appeal to a man as a creative artist making his soul. To say to a man, "rascal" or "villain" in ordinary society may seem abrupt; but it is also elliptical. It is an abbreviation of a sublime spiritual apostrophe for which there may be no time in our busy social life. When you meet a millionaire, the cornerer of many markets, out at dinner in Mayfair, and greet him (as is your custom) with the exclamation "Scoundrel!" you are merely shortening for convenience some such expression as: "How can you, having the divine spirit of man that might be higher than the angels, drag it down so far as to be a scoundrel?" When you are introduced at a garden party to a Cabinet Minister who takes tips on Government contracts, and when you say to him in the ordinary way "Scamp!" you are merely using the last word of a long moral disquisition; which is in effect, "How pathetic is the spiritual spectacle of this Cabinet Minister, who being from the first made glorious by the image of God, condescends so far to lesser ambitions as to allow them to turn him into a scamp." It is a mere taking of the tail of a sentence to stand for the rest; like saying 'bus for omnibus. It is even more like the case of that seventeenth century Puritan whose name was something like "If-Jesus-Christ-Had-Not-Died-For-Thee-Thou-Hadst-Been-Damned Higgins"; but who was, for popular convenience, referred to as "Damned Higgins." But it is obvious, anyhow, that when we call a man a coward, we are in so doing asking him how he can be a coward when he could be a hero. When we rebuke a man for being a sinner, we imply that he has the powers of a saint.

But punishing him for the protection of society involves no regard for him at all. It involves no limit of proportion in the punishment at all. There are some limits to what ordinary men are likely to say that an ordinary man deserves. But there are no limits to what the danger of the community may be supposed to demand. We would not, even if we could, boil the millionaire in oil or skin the poor little politician alive; for we do not think a man deserves to be skinned alive for taking commissions on contracts. But it is by no means so certain that the skinning him

G. K. CHESTERTON

alive might not protect the community. Corruption can destroy communities; and torture can deter men. At any rate the thing is not so self-evidently useless as it is self-evidently unjust and vindictive. We refrain from such fantastic punishments, largely because we *do* have some notion of making the punishment fit the crime, and not merely fit the community. If the State were the sole consideration, it may be inferred a priori that people might be much more cruel. And in fact, where the State was the sole consideration, it was found in experience that they were much more cruel. They were much more cruel precisely because they were freed from all responsibilities about the innocence or guilt of the individual. I believe that in heathen Rome, the model of a merely civic and secular loyalty, it was a common practice to torture the slaves of any household subjected to legal enquiry. If you had remonstrated, because no crime had been proved against the slaves, the State would had answered in the modern manner: "We are not punishing the crime; we are protecting the community."

Now that example is relevant just now in more ways than one. Of course I do not mean that this was the motive of all historical cruelties, or that some did not spring from quite an opposite motive. But it was the motive of much tyranny in the heathen world; and in this, as in other things, the modern world has largely become a heathen world. And modern tyranny can find its prototype in the torturing of heathen slaves in two fundamental respects. First, that the modern world has returned to the test of the heathen world, that of considering service to the state and not justice to the individual. And second, that the modern world, like the heathen world, is here inflicting it chiefly on subordinate and submerged classes of society; on slaves or those who are almost slaves.

For the heathen state is a Servile State. And no one has more of this view of the state than the State Socialists. The official Labour Politician would be the first to say in theory that punishment must not be a moral recompense, but merely a social regulation. And he would be the first to say in practice that it is the poor and ignorant who must be regulated. Doubtless it is one thing to be regulated and another to be tortured. But when once the principle is admitted broadly, the progress towards torture may proceed pretty briskly. In the psychological sphere, it is already as bad as it has ever been. It may come as a surprise to the humanitarian to learn it; but it is none the less true, that a mother may undergo moral torture in the last degree, when her children are taken from her by brute force. And that incident has become so common in the policing of the poor nowadays as hardly to call for notice. And that example is particularly relevant to the present argument. Nobody could pretend that the affectionate mother of a rather backward child *deserves* to be punished by having all the happiness taken out of her life. But anybody can pretend that the act is needed for the happiness of the community. Nobody will say it was so wicked of her to love her baby

G. K. CHESTERTON

that she deserves to lose it. But it is always easy to say that some remote social purpose will be served by taking it away. Thus the elimination of punishment means the extension of tyranny. Men would not do things so oppressive so long as they were vindictive. It is only when punishment is purged of vengeance that it can be as villainous as that.

For that matter, it would be easy to find examples much nearer than this one to the torturing of the Roman slaves. There is a very close parallel in the Third Degree, as applied by the police to the criminal class on suspicion, especially in America; for the criminal class is a submerged class like the slaves; and it is but an experiment on the nerves in one way instead of another, like a preference for the rack rather than the thumbscrew. But the point is that it is applied to the criminal type without any proof that it is in this case criminal; and the thing is justified not by the criminality of the individual but by the needs of the State. The police would answer exactly as the pagans answered: "We are not punishing the crime; we are protecting the community."

This tyranny is spreading. And there is no hope for liberty or democracy until we all demand again, with a tongue of thunder, the right to be blamed. We shall never feel like free men until we assert again our sacred claim to be punished. The denunciation of a man for what he chose to do is itself the confession that he chose to do it; and it is beneath his dignity to admit that he could have done nothing else. The only alternative theory is that we can do nothing but what we do, and our rulers can do anything whatever to restrain us. Compared with that, it would be better that roaring mobs should rise all over England, uproariously demanding to be hanged.

A DEFENCE OF DRAMATIC UNITIES

Injustice is done to the old classical rules of artistic criticism, because we do not treat them as artistic criticism. We first turn them into police regulations, and then complain of them for being so. But I suspect, with the submission proper to ignorance, that the art canons of Aristotle and others were much more generally artistic, in the sense of atmospheric. We allow a romantic critic to be as dogmatic as Ruskin, and still feel that he is not really being so despotic as Boileau. If a modern, like Maeterlinck, says that all drama is in an open door at the end of an empty passage, we do not take it literally, like a notice requiring an extra exit in case of fire. But if an ancient, like Horace, says that all drama demands a closed door, which shall hide Medea while she murders her children, then we do receive it as something rigid and formal, like the order to close the shutters on Zeppelin nights. Now how far the classical critics took their rules absolutely I do not know. But I am substantially sure that there is a true instinct at the back of them, whatever exceptions be allowed at the edges. The unities of time and place, that is the idea of keeping figures and events within the frame of a few hours or a few yards, is naturally derided as a specially artificial affront to the intellect. But I am sure it is especially true suggestion to the imagination. It is exactly in the artistic atmosphere, where rules and reasons are so hard to define, that this unification would be most easy to defend. This limitation to a few scenes and actors really has something in it that pleases the imagination and not the reason. There are instances in which it may be broken boldly; there are types of art to which it does not apply at all. But wherever it can be satisfied, something not superficial but rather subconscious is satisfied. Something re-visits us that is the strange soul of single places; the shadow of haunting ghosts or of household gods. Like all such things, it is indescribable when it is successful: it is easier to describe the disregard of it as unsuccessful. Thus Stevenson's masterpiece, "The Master of Ballantrae," always seems to me to fall into two parts, the finer which revolves round Durisdeer and the inferior which rambles through India and America. The slender and sinister figure in black, standing on the shore or vanishing from the shrubbery, does really seem to have come from the ends of the earth. In the chapters of travel he only serves to show that, for a boy's adventure tale, a good villain makes a bad hero. And even about Hamlet I am so heretical as to be almost classical; I doubt whether the exile in England does not rather dwarf than dignify the prisoner of Denmark. I am not sure that he got anything out of the pirates he could not have got out of the players. And I am very sure indeed that this figure in black, like the other, produces a

G. K. CHESTERTON

true though intangible effect of tragedy when, and because, we see him against the great grey background of the house of his fathers. In a word, it is what Mr. J. B. Yeats, the poet's stimulating parent, calls in his excellent book of essays "the drama of the home." The drama is domestic, and is dramatic because it is domestic.

We might say that superior literature is centripetal, while inferior literature is centrifugal. But oddly enough, the same truth may be found by studying inferior as well as superior literature. What is true of a Shakespearian play is equally true of a shilling shocker. The shocker is at its worst when it wanders and escapes through new scenes and new characters. The shocker is at its best when it shocks by something familiar; a figure or fact that is already known though not understood. A good detective story also can keep the classic unities; or otherwise play the game. I for one devour detective stories; I am delighted when the dagger of the curate is found to be the final clue to the death of the vicar. But there is a point of honour for the author; he may conceal the curate's crime, but he must not conceal the curate. I feel I am cheated when the last chapter hints for the first time that the vicar had a curate. I am annoyed when a curate, who is a total stranger to me, is produced from a cupboard or a box in a style at once abrupt and belated. I am annoyed most of all when the new curate is only the tool of a terrible secret society ramifying from Moscow or Thibet. These cosmopolitan complications are the dull and not the dramatic element in the ingenious tales of Mr. Oppenheim or Mr. Le Queux. They entirely spoil the fine domesticity of a good murder. It is unsportsmanlike to call spies from the end of the earth, as it is to call spirits from the vasty deep, in a story that does not imply them from the start. And this because the supply is infinite; and the infinite, as Coventry Patmore well said, is generally alien to art. Everybody knows that the universe contains enough spies or enough spectres to kill the most healthy and vigorous vicar. The drama of detection is in discovering how he can be killed decently and economically, within the classic unities of time and place. In short, the good mystery story should narrow its circles like an eagle about to swoop. The spiral should curve inwards and not outwards. And this inward movement is in true poetic mysteries as well as mere police mystifications. It will be assumed that I am joking if I say there is a serious social meaning in this novel-reader's notion of keeping a crime in the family. It must seem mere nonsense to find a moral in this fancy, about washing gory linen at home. It will naturally be asked whether I have idealized the home merely as a good place for assassinations. I have not; any more than I have idealized the Church as a thing in which the curates can kill the vicars. Nevertheless the thing, like many things, is symbolic though it is not serious. And the objection to it implies a subtle misunderstanding, in many minds, of the whole case for the home as I have

G. K. CHESTERTON

sometimes had occasion to urge it. When we defend the family we do not mean it is always a peaceful family; when we maintain the thesis of marriage we do not mean that it is always a happy marriage. We mean that it is the theatre of the spiritual drama, the place where things happen, especially the things that matter. It is not so much the place where a man kills his wife as the place where he can take the equally sensational step of not killing his wife. There is truth in the cynicism that calls marriage a trial; but even the cynic will admit that a trial may end in an acquittal. And the reason that the family has this central and crucial character is the same reason that makes it in politics the only prop of liberty. The family is the test of freedom; because the family is the only thing that the free man makes for himself and by himself. Other institutions must largely be made for him by strangers, whether the institutions be despotic or democratic. There is no other way of organizing mankind which can give this power and dignity, not only to mankind but to men. If anybody likes to put it so, we cannot really make all men democrats unless we make all men despots. That is to say, the co-operation of the commonwealth will be a mere automatic unanimity like that of insects, unless the citizen has some province of purely voluntary action; unless he is so far not only a citizen but a king. In the world of ethics this is called liberty; in the world of economics it is called property, and in the world of æsthetics, necessarily so much more dim and indefinable, it is darkly adumbrated in the old dramatic unities of place or time. It must indeed be a mistake in any case to treat such artistic rules as rigidly as if they were moral rules. It was an error if they ever were so treated; it may well be a question whether they were ever meant to be so treated. But when critics have suggested that these classical canons were a mere superficial varnish, it may safely be said that it is the critics who are superficial. Modern artists would have been wiser if they had developed sympathetically some of the Aristotelian æsthetics, as mediæval philosophers developed sympathetically the Aristotelian logic and ethics. For a more subtle study of the unities of time and place, for example, as outlined for the Greek drama, might have led us towards what is perhaps the last secret of all legend and literature. It might have suggested why poets, pagan or not, returned perpetually to the idea of happiness as a place for humanity as a person. It might suggest why the world is always seeking for absolutes that are not abstractions; why fairyland was always a land, and even the Superman was almost a man.

G. K. CHESTERTON

THE BOREDOM OF BUTTERFLIES

There is one thing which critics perhaps tend to forget when they complain that Mr. H. G. Wells no longer concerns himself with telling a story. It is that nobody else could interest and excite us so much without telling a story. It is possible to read one of his recent novels almost without knowing the story at all. It is possible to dip into it as into a book of essays, and pick up opinions here and there. But all the essays are brilliant essays, and all the opinions are striking opinions. It does not much matter who holds the opinions; it is possible that the author does not hold them at all, and pretty certain that he will not hold them long. But nobody else could make such splendid stuff out of the very refuse of his rejected opinions. Seen from this side, even what is called his failure must be recognized as a remarkable success. The personal story may fade away, but it is something of an achievement to be still interesting after becoming impersonal; like the achievement of the Cheshire cat who could grin when he was no longer there. Moreover, these impersonal and even irresponsible opinions of Mr. Wells, though never conclusive, are always suggestive; each is a good starting-point for thought, if only for the thought that refutes it. In short, the critics of Mr. Wells rather exaggerate the danger of his story running to speculation, as if it were merely running to seed. Anyhow, they ought to remember that there are two meanings in running to seed; and one of them is connected with seed-time.

I have, however, a particular reason for mentioning the matter here. I confess there is more than one of Mr. Wells's recent novels that I have both read and not read. I am never quite sure that I have read all Shakespeare or all Boswell's Johnson; because I have so long had the habit of opening them anywhere. So I have opened the works of Mr. Wells anywhere, and had great fun out of the essays that would have seemed only long parentheses in the story. But, on getting to rather closer grips with the last of his stories, "The Secret Places of the Heart," I think I have caught a glimpse of a difficulty in this sort of narrative which is something deeper than mere digression. In a story like "Pickwick" or "Tristram Shandy" digression is never disappointment. But in this case, differing as I do from the merely hostile critics, I cannot dispel the atmosphere of disappointment. The story seems inconclusive in a sense beyond anything merely inconsistent; and I fancy I can guess why.

A pedantic logician may perhaps imagine that a thing can only be inconclusive at the conclusion. But I will boldly claim the liberty in language of saying that this sort of thing is inconclusive from the start. It begins inconclusive, and in that sense begins dull. The hero begins by telling the doctor about a mutable flux of flirtation, about his own experiments as a philanderer, always flitting like a butterfly from flower

G. K. CHESTERTON

to flower. Now, it is highly probable that the diary of a butterfly would be very dull, even if it were only the diary of a day. His round need be no more really amusing than a postman's, since he has no serious spiritual interest in any of his places of call. Now, by starting his hero as a philosopher and also philanderer, and taking seriously his philosophy of philandering, the author as good as tells us, to start with, that his hero will not have any serious adventures at all. At the beginning of the story, he practically tells us that there will be no story. The story of a fickle man is not a story at all; because there is no strain or resistance in it. Somebody talked about tales with a twist; and it is certain that all tales are tales with a tug.

All the most subtle truths of literature are to be found in legend. There is no better test of the truth of serious fiction than the simple truths to be found in a fairy tale or an old ballad. Now, in the whole of folk-lore there is no such thing as free love. There is such a thing as false love. There is also another thing, which the old ballads always talk of as true love. But the story always turns on the keeping of a bond or the breaking of it; and this quite apart from orthodox morality in the matter of the marriage bond. The love may be in the strict sense sinful, but it is never anarchical. There was quite as little freedom for Lancelot as for Arthur; quite as little mere philandering in the philosophy of Tristram as in the philosophy of Galahad. It may have been unlawful love, but it certainly was not lawless love. In the old ballads there is the triumph of true love, as in "The Bailiff's Daughter of Islington"; or the tragedy of true love, as in "Helen of Kirkconnel Lea"; or the tragedy of false love, as in the ballad of "Oh waly, waly up the bank." But there is neither triumph nor tragedy in the idea of *avowedly* transient love; and no literature will ever be made out of it, except the very lightest literature of satire. And even the satire must be a satire on fickleness, and therefore involve an indirect ideal of fidelity. But you cannot make any enduring literature out of love *conscious* that it will not endure. Even if this mutability were working as morality, it would still be unworkable as art.

The decadents used to say that things like the marriage vow might be very convenient for commonplace public purposes, but had no place in the world of beauty and imagination. The truth is exactly the other way. The truth is that if marriage had not existed it would have been necessary for artists to invent it. The truth is that if constancy had never been needed as a social requirement, it would still have been created out of cloud and air as a poetical requirement. If ever monogamy is abandoned in practice, it will linger in legend and in literature. When society is haunted by the butterfly flitting from flower to flower, poetry will still be describing the desire of the moth for the star; and it will be a fixed star. Literature must always revolve round loyalties; for a rudimentary psychological reason, which is simply the nature of narrative. You cannot tell a *story*

G. K. CHESTERTON

without the idea of pursuing a purpose and sticking to a point. You cannot tell a story without the idea of the Quest, the idea of the Vow; even if it be only the idea of the Wager.

Perhaps the most modern equivalent to the man who makes a vow is the man who makes a bet. But he must not hedge on a bet; still less must he welsh, or do a bolt when he has made a bet. Even if the story ends with his doing so, the dramatic emotion depends on our realizing the dishonesty of his doing so. That is, the drama depends on the keeping or breaking of a bond, if it be only a bet. A man wandering about a race-course, making bets that nobody took seriously, would be merely a bore. And so the hero wandering through a novel, making vows of love that nobody took seriously, is merely a bore. The point here is not so much that morally it cannot be a creditable story, but that artistically it cannot be a story at all. Art is born when the temporary touches the eternal; the shock of beauty is when the irresistible force hits the immovable post.

Thus in the last novel of Mr. Wells, what is inconclusive in the second part is largely due to what is convincing in the first part. By the time that the hero meets his new heroine on Salisbury Plain, he has seriously convinced us that there is nothing heroic about him, and that nothing heroic will happen to him; at any rate in that department. He disenchants the enchantment beforehand, and warns the reader against even a momentary illusion. When once a man looks forward as well as backward to disillusionment, no romance can be made of him.

Profligacy may be made romantic, precisely because it implies some betrayal or breaking of a law. But polygamy is not in the least romantic. Polygamy is dull to the point of respectability. When a man looks forward to a number of wives as he does to a number of cigarettes, you can no more make a book out of them than out of the bills from his tobacconist. Anything having the character of a Turkish harem has also something of the character of a Turkey carpet. It is not a portrait, or even a picture, but a pattern. We may at the moment be looking at one highly coloured and even flamboyant figure in the carpet; but we know that on every side, in front as well as behind, the image is repeated without purpose and without finality.

THE TERROR OF A TOY

It would be too high and hopeful a compliment to say that the world is becoming absolutely babyish. For its chief weak-mindedness is an inability to appreciate the intelligence of babies. On every side we hear whispers and warnings that would have appeared half-witted to the Wise Men of Gotham. Only this Christmas I was told in a toy-shop that not so many bows and arrows were being made for little boys; because they were considered dangerous. It might in some circumstances be dangerous to have a little bow. It is always dangerous to have a little boy. But no other society, claiming to be sane, would have dreamed of supposing that you could abolish all bows unless you could abolish all boys. With the merits of the latter reform I will not deal here. There is a great deal to be said for such a course; and perhaps we shall soon have an opportunity of considering it. For the modern mind seems quite incapable of distinguishing between the means and the end, between the organ and the disease, between the use and the abuse; and would doubtless break the boy along with the bow, as it empties out the baby with the bath.

But let us, by way of a little study in this mournful state of things, consider this case of the dangerous toy. Now the first and most self-evident truth is that, of all the things a child sees and touches, the most dangerous toy is about the least dangerous thing. There is hardly a single domestic utensil that is not much more dangerous than a little bow and arrows. He can burn himself in the fire, he can boil himself in the bath, he can cut his throat with the carving-knife, he can scald himself with the kettle, he can choke himself with anything small enough, he can break his neck off anything high enough. He moves all day long amid a murderous machinery, as capable of killing and maiming as the wheels of the most frightful factory. He plays all day in a house fitted up with engines of torture like the Spanish Inquisition. And while he thus dances in the shadow of death, he is to be saved from all the perils of possessing a piece of string, tied to a bent bough or twig. When he is a little boy it generally takes him some time even to learn how to hold the bow. When he does hold it, he is delighted if the arrow flutters for a few yards like a feather or an autumn leaf. But even if he grows a little older and more skilful, and has yet not learned to despise arrows in favour of aeroplanes, the amount of damage he could conceivably do with his little arrows would be about one-hundredth part of the damage that he could always in any case have done by simply picking up a stone in the garden.

Now you do not keep a little boy from throwing stones by preventing him from ever seeing stones. You do not do it by locking up all the stones in the Geological Museum, and only issuing tickets of admission to adults. You do not do it by trying to pick

G. K. CHESTERTON

up all the pebbles on the beach, for fear he should practise throwing them into the sea. You do not even adopt so obvious and even pressing a social reform as forbidding roads to be made of anything but asphalt, or directing that all gardens shall be made on clay and none on gravel. You neglect all these great opportunities opening before you; you neglect all these inspiring vistas of social science and enlightenment. When you want to prevent a child from throwing stones, you fall back on the stalest and most sentimental and even most superstitious methods. You do it by trying to preserve some reasonable authority and influence over the child. You trust to your private relation with the boy, and not to your public relation with the stone. And what is true of the natural missile is just as true, of course, of the artificial missile; especially as it is a very much more ineffectual and therefore innocuous missile. A man could be really killed, like St. Stephen, with the stones in the road. I doubt if he could be really killed, like St. Sebastian, with the arrows in the toy-shop. But anyhow the very plain principle is the same. If you can teach a child not to throw a stone, you can teach him when to shoot an arrow; if you cannot teach him anything, he will always have something to throw. If he can be persuaded not to smash the Archdeacon's hat with a heavy flint, it will probably be possible to dissuade him from transfixing that head-dress with a toy arrow. If his training deters him from heaving half a brick at the postman, it will probably also warn him against constantly loosening shafts of death against the policeman. But the notion that the child depends upon particular implements, labelled dangerous, in order to be a danger to himself and other people, is a notion so nonsensical that it is hard to see how any human mind can entertain it for a moment. The truth is that all sorts of faddism, both official and theoretical, have broken down the natural authority of the domestic institution, especially among the poor; and the faddists are now casting about desperately for a substitute for the thing they have themselves destroyed. The normal thing is for the parents to prevent a boy from doing more than a reasonable amount of damage with his bow and arrow; and for the rest, to leave him to a reasonable enjoyment of them. Officialism cannot thus follow the life of the individual boy, as can the individual guardian. You cannot appoint a particular policeman for each boy, to pursue him when he climbs trees or falls into ponds. So the modern spirit has descended to the indescribable mental degradation of trying to abolish the abuse of things by abolishing the things themselves; which is as if it were to abolish ponds or abolish trees. Perhaps it will have a try at that before long. Thus we have all heard of savages who try a tomahawk for murder, or burn a wooden club for the damage it has done to society. To such intellectual levels may the world return.

There are indeed yet lower levels. There is a story from America about a little boy who gave up his toy cannon to assist the disarmament of the world. I do

G. K. CHESTERTON

not know if it is true, but on the whole I prefer to think so; for it is perhaps more tolerable to imagine one small monster who could do such a thing than many more mature monsters who could invent or admire it. There were some doubtless who neither invented nor admired. It is one of the peculiarities of the Americans that they combine a power of producing what they satirize as "sobstuff" with a parallel power of satirizing it. And of the two American tall stories, it is sometimes hard to say which is the story and which the satire. But it seems clear that some people did really repeat this story in a reverential spirit. And it marks, as I have said, another stage of cerebral decay. You can (with luck) break a window with a toy arrow; but you can hardly bombard a town with a toy gun. If people object to the mere model of a cannon, they must equally object to the picture of a cannon, and so to every picture in the world that depicts a sword or a spear. There would be a splendid clearance of all the great art-galleries of the world. But it would be nothing to the destruction of all the great libraries of the world, if we logically extended the principle to all the literary masterpieces that admit the glory of arms. When this progress had gone on for a century or two, it might begin to dawn on people that there was something wrong with their moral principle. What is wrong with their moral principle is that it is immoral. Arms, like every other adventure or art of man, have two sides according as they are invoked for the infliction or the defiance of wrong. They have also an element of real poetry and an element of realistic and therefore repulsive prose. The child's symbolic sword and bow are simply the poetry without the prose; the good without the evil. The toy sword is the abstraction and emanation of the heroic, apart from all its horrible accidents. It is the soul of the sword, that will never be stained with blood.

FALSE THEORY AND THE THEATRE

A theatrical manager recently insisted on introducing Chinese labour into the theatrical profession. He insisted on having real Chinamen to take the part of Chinese servants; and some actors seem to have resented it—as I think, very reasonably. A distinguished actress, who is clever enough to know better, defended it on the ground that nothing must interfere with the perfection of a work of art. I dispute the moral thesis in any case; and Nero would no doubt have urged it in defence of having real deaths in the amphitheatre. I do not admit in any case that the artist can be entirely indifferent to hunger and unemployment, any more than to lions or boiling oil. But, as a matter of fact, there is no need to raise the moral question, because the case is equally strong in relation to the artistic question. I do not think that a Chinese character being represented by a Chinese actor is the finishing touch to the perfection of a work of art. I think it is the last and lowest phase of the vulgarity that is called realism. It is in the same style and taste as the triumphs on which, I believe, some actor-managers have prided themselves: the triumphs of having real silver for goblets or real jewels for crowns. That is not the spirit of a perfect artist, but rather of a purse-proud parvenu. The perfect artist would be he who could put on a crown of gilt wire or tinsel and make us feel he was a king.

Moreover, if the principle is to be extended from properties to persons, it is not easy to see where the principle can stop. If we are to insist on real Asiatics to act "Chu Chin Chow," why not insist on real Venetians to act "The Merchant of Venice"? We did experiment recently, and I believe very successfully, in having the Jew acted by a real Jew. But I hardly think we should like to make it a rule that nobody must be allowed to act Shylock unless he can prove his racial right to call upon his father Abraham. Must the characters of Macbeth and Macduff only be represented by men with names like Macpherson and Macnab? Must the Prince of Denmark be native there and to the manner born? Must we import a crowd of Greeks before we are allowed to act "Troilus and Cressida," or a mob of real Egyptians to form the background of "Antony and Cleopatra"? Will it be necessary to kidnap an African gentleman out of Africa, by the methods of the slave trade, and force him into acting Othello? It was rather foolishly suggested at one time that our allies in Japan might be offended at the fantastic satire of "The Mikado." As a matter of fact, the satire of "The Mikado" is not at all directed against Japanese things, but exclusively against English things. But I certainly think there might be some little ill-feeling in Japan if gangs of Japanese coolies were shipped across two continents merely in order to act in it. If once this singular rule

G. K. CHESTERTON

be recognized, a dramatist will certainly be rather shy of introducing Zulus or Red Indians into his dramas, owing to the difficulty in securing appropriate dramatic talent. He will hesitate before making his hero an Eskimo. He will abandon his intention of seeking his heroine in the Sandwich Islands. If he were to insist on introducing real cannibals, it seems possible that they might insist on introducing real cannibalism. This would be quite in the spirit of Nero and all the art critics of the Roman realism of the amphitheatre. But surely it would be putting almost too perfect a finishing touch to the perfection of a work of art. That kind of finishing touch is a little too finishing.

The irony grew more intense when the newspapers that had insisted on Chinamen because they could not help being Chinamen began to praise them with admiration and astonishment because they looked Chinese. This opens up a speculation so complex and contradictory that I do not propose to follow it, for I am interested here not in the particular incident but in the general idea. It will be a sufficient statement of the fundamental fact of all the arts if I say simply that I do not believe in the resemblance. I do not believe that a Chinaman does look like a Chinaman. That is, I do not believe that any Chinaman will necessarily look like *the* Chinaman—the Chinaman in the imagination of the artist and the interest of the crowd. We all know the fable of the man who imitated a pig, and his rival who was hooted by the crowd because he could only produce what was (in fact) the squeak of a real pig. The crowd was perfectly right. The crowd was a crowd of very penetrating and philosophical art critics. They had come there not to hear an ordinary pig, which they could hear by poking in any ordinary pigsty. They had come to hear how the voice of the pig affects the immortal mind and spirit of man; what sort of satire he would make of it; what sort of fun he can get out of it; what sort of exaggeration he feels to be an exaggeration of its essence, and not of its accidents. In other words, they had come to hear a squeak, but the sort of squeak which expresses what a man thinks of a pig—not the vastly inferior squeak which only expresses what a pig thinks of a man. I have myself a poetical enthusiasm for pigs, and the paradise of my fancy is one where the pigs have wings. But it is only men, especially wise men, who discuss whether pigs can fly; we have no particular proof that pigs ever discuss it. Therefore the actor who imitated the quadruped may well have put into his squeak something of the pathetic cry of one longing for the wings of the dove. The quadruped himself might express no such sentiment; he might appear, and generally does appear, singularly unconscious of his own lack of feathers. But the same principle is true of things more dignified than the most dignified porker, though clad in the most superb plumage. If a vision of a stately Arab has risen in the imagination of an author who is an artist, he will be wise if he confides it to an actor who

G. K. CHESTERTON

is also an artist. He will be much wiser to confide it to an actor than to an Arab. The actor, being a fellow-countryman and a fellow-artist, may bring out what the author thinks the Arab stands for; whereas the real Arab might be a particular individual who at that particular moment refused to stand for anything of the sort, or for anything at all. The principle is a general one; and I mean no disrespect to China in the porcine parallel, or in the figurative association of pigs and pigtails.

But, as a matter of fact, the argument is especially apt in the case of China. For I fear that China is chiefly interesting to most of us as the other end of the world. It is valued as something far-off, and therefore fantastical, like a kingdom in the clouds of sunrise. It is not the very real virtues of the Chinese tradition—its stoicism, its sense of honour, its ancient peasant cults—that most people want to put into a play. It is the ordinary romantic feeling about something remote and extravagant, like the Martians or the Man in the Moon. It is perfectly reasonable to have that romantic feeling in moderation, like other amusements. But it is not reasonable to expect the remote person to feel remote from himself, or the man at the other end of the world not to feel it as this end. We must not ask the outlandish Oriental to feel outlandish, or a Chinaman to be astonished at being Chinese. If, therefore, the literary artist has the legitimate literary purpose of expressing the mysterious and alien atmosphere which China implies to him, he will probably do it much better with the aid of an actor who is not Chinese. Of course, I am not criticizing the particular details of the particular performance, of which I know little or nothing. I do not know the circumstances; and under the circumstances, for all I know, the experiment may have been very necessary or very successful. I merely protest against a theory of dramatic truth, urged in defence of the dramatic experiment, which seems to me calculated to falsify the whole art of the drama. It is founded on exactly the same fallacy as that of the infant in Stevenson's nursery rhyme, who thought that the Japanese children must suffer from home-sickness through being always abroad in Japan.

This brings us very near to an old and rather threadbare theatrical controversy, about whether staging should be simple or elaborate. I do not mean to begin that argument all over again. What is really wanted is not so much the simple stage-manager as the simple spectator. In a very real sense, what is wanted is the simple critic, who would be in truth the most subtle critic. The healthy human instincts in these things are at least as much spoiled by sophistication in the stalls as by elaboration on the stage. A really simple mind would enjoy a simple scene—and also a gorgeous scene. A popular instinct, to be found in all folklore, would know well enough when the one or the other was appropriate. But what is involved here is not the whole of that sophistication, but only one particular sophistry, and against that sophistry

G. K. CHESTERTON

we may well pause to protest. It is the critical fallacy of cutting off a real donkey's head to put it on Bottom the Weaver; when the head is symbolical, and in that case more appropriate to the critic than to the actor.

THE SECRET SOCIETY OF MANKIND

With that fantastic love of paradox which gives pain to so many critics, I once suggested that there may be some truth in the notion of the brotherhood of men. This was naturally a subject for severe criticism from the modern or modernist standpoint; and I remember that the cleverest refutation of it occurred in a book which was called "We Moderns." It was written by Mr. Edward Moore, and very well written too; indeed the author did himself some injustice in insisting on his own modernity; for he was not so very modern after all, but really quite lucid and coherent. But I will venture to take his remark as a text here because it concerns a matter on which most moderns darken counsel in a highly incoherent manner. It concerns the nature of the unity of men; which I did certainly state in its more defiant form as the equality of man. And I said that this norm or meeting-place of mankind can be found in the two extremes of the comic and the tragic. I said that no individual tragedy could be so tragic as having to die; and all men have equally to die. I said that nothing can be funnier than having two legs; and all men can join equally in the joke.

The critic in question was terribly severe on this remark. I believe that the words of his condemnation ran as follows: "Well, in this passage, there is an error so plain, it is almost inconceivable that a responsible thinker could have put it forward even in jest. For it is clear that the tragic and comic elements of which Mr. Chesterton speaks make not only mankind, but *all life*, equal. Everything that lives must die; and therefore it is, in Mr. Chesterton's sense, tragic. Everything that lives has shape; and therefore it is, in Mr. Chesterton's sense, comic. His premises lead to the equality not of mankind, but of all that lives; whether it be leviathan or butterfly, oak or violet, worm or eagle.... Would that he had said this! Then we who affirm inequality would be the first to echo him." I do not feel it hard to show that where Mr. Moore thinks equality wrong is exactly where it is right; and I will begin with mortality; premising that the same is true (for those who believe it) of immortality. Both are absolutes: a man cannot be somewhat mortal; nor can he be rather immortal.

To begin with, it must be understood that having an equality in being black or white is not even the same as being equally black or white. It is generally fair to take a familiar illustration; and I will take the ordinary expression about being all in the same boat. Mr. Moore and I and all men are not only all in the same boat, but have a very real equality implied in that fact. Nevertheless, since there is a word "inner" as well as a word "in," there is a sense in which some of us might be more in the boat than others. My fellow passengers might have stowed me at the bottom of the boat and sat on top of me, moved by a natural

G. K. CHESTERTON

distaste for my sitting on top of them. I have noticed that I am often thus packed in a preliminary fashion into the back seats or basic parts of cabs, cars, or boats; there being evidently a feeling that I am the stuff of which the foundations of an edifice are made rather than its toppling minarets or tapering spires. Meanwhile Mr. Moore might be surveying the world from the masthead, if there were one, or leaning out over the prow with the forward gestures of a leader of men, or even sitting by preference on the edge of the boat with his feet paddling in the water, to indicate the utmost possible aristocratic detachment from us and our concerns. Nevertheless, in the large and ultimate matters which are the whole meaning of the phrase "all in the same boat," we should be all equally in the same boat. We should be all equally dependent upon the reassuring fact that a boat can float. If it did not float but sink, each one of us would have lost his one and only boat at the same decisive time and in the same disconcerting manner. If the King of the Cannibal Islands, upon whose principal island we might suffer the inconvenience of being wrecked, were to exclaim in a loud voice "I will eat every single man who has arrived by that identical boat and no other," we should all be eaten, and we should all be equally eaten. For being eaten, considered as a tragedy, is not a matter of degree.

Now there is a fault in every analogy; but the fault in my analogy is not a fault in my argument; it is the chief fault in Mr. Moore's argument. It may be said that even in a shipwreck men are not equal, for some of us might be so strong that we could swim to the shore, or some of us might be so tough that the island king would repent of his rash vow after the first bite. But it is precisely here that I have again, as delicately as possible, to draw the reader's attention to the modest and little-known institution called death. We are all in a boat which will certainly drown us all, and drown us equally, the strongest with the weakest; we sail to the land of an ogre, *edax rerum*, who devours all without distinction. And the meaning in the phrase about being all in the same boat is, not that there are no degrees among the people in a boat, but that all those degrees are nothing compared with the stupendous fact that the boat goes home or goes down. And it is when I come to the particular criticism on my remarks about "the fact of having to die" that I feel most confident that I was right and that Mr. Moore is wrong.

It will be noted that I spoke of the fact of having to die, not of the fact of dying. The brotherhood of men, being a spiritual thing, is not concerned merely with the truth that all men will die, but with the truth that all men know it. It is true, as Mr. Moore says, that everything will die, "whether it be leviathan or butterfly, oak or violet, worm or eagle"; but exactly what, at the very start, we do not know is whether they know it. Can Mr. Moore draw forth leviathan with a hook, and extract his hopes and fears about the heavenly harpooner? Can he worm its philosophy out of a

G. K. CHESTERTON

worm, or get the caterpillar to talk about the faint possibility of a butterfly? The caterpillar on the leaf may repeat to Blake his mother's grief; but it does not repeat to anybody its own grief about its own mother. Can he know whether oaks confront their fate with hearts of oak, as the phrase is used in a sailor's song? He cannot; and this is the whole point about human brotherhood, the point the vegetarians cannot see. This is why a harpooner is not an assassin; this is why eating whale's blubber, though not attractive to the fancy, is not repulsive to the conscience. We do not know what a whale thinks of death; still less what the other whales think of his being killed and eaten. He may be a pessimistic whale, and be perpetually wishing that this too, too solid blubber would melt, thaw and resolve itself into a dew. He may be a fanatical whale, and feel frantically certain of passing instantly into a polar paradise of whales, ruled by the sacred whale who swallowed Jonah. But we can elicit no sign or gesture from him suggestive of such reflections; and the working common sense of the thing is that no creatures outside man seem to have any sense of death at all. Mr. Moore has therefore chosen a strangely unlucky point upon which to challenge the true egalitarian doctrine. Almost the most arresting and even startling stamp of the solidarity and sameness of mankind is precisely this fact, not only of death, but of the shadow of death. We do know of any man whatever what we do not know of any other thing whatever, that his death is what we call a tragedy. From the fact that it is a tragedy flow all the forms and tests by which we say it is a murder or an execution, a martyrdom or a suicide. They all depend on an echo or vibration, not only in the soul of man, but in the souls of all men.

Oddly enough, Mr. Moore has made exactly the same mistake about the comic as about the tragic. It is true, I think, that almost everything which has a shape is humorous; but it is not true that everything which has a shape has a sense of humour. The whale may be laughable, but it is not the whale who laughs; the image indeed is almost alarming. And the instant the question is raised, we collide with another colossal fact, dwarfing all human differentiations; the fact that man is the only creature who does laugh. In the presence of this prodigious fact, the fact that men laugh in different degrees, and at different things, shrivels not merely into insignificance but into invisibility. It is true that I have often felt the physical universe as something like a firework display: the most practical of all practical jokes. But if the cosmos is meant for a joke, men seem to be the only cosmic conspirators who have been let into the joke. There could be no fraternity like our freemasonry in that secret pleasure. It is true that there are no limits to this jesting faculty, that it is not confined to common human jests; but it is confined to human jesters. Mr. Moore may burst out laughing when he beholds the morning star, or be thrown into convulsions of amusement by the effect of moonrise

G. K. CHESTERTON

seen through a mist. He may, to quote his own catalogue, see all the fun of an eagle or an oak tree. We may come upon him in some quiet dell rolling about in uproarious mirth at the sight of a violet. But we shall not find the violet in a state of uproarious mirth at Mr. Moore. He may laugh at the worm; but the worm will not turn and laugh at him. For that comfort he must come to his fellow-sinners: I shall always be ready to oblige.

The truth involved here has had many names; that man is the image of God; that he is the microcosm; that he is the measure of all things. He is the microcosm in the sense that he is the mirror, the only crystal we know in which the fantasy and fear in things are, in the double and real sense, things of reflection. In the presence of this mysterious monopoly the differences of men are like dust. That is what the equality of men means to me; and that is the only intelligible thing it ever meant to anybody. The common things of men infinitely outclass all classes. For a man to disagree with this it is necessary that he should understand it; Mr. Moore may really disagree with it; but the ordinary modern anti-egalitarian does not understand it, or apparently anything else. If a man says he had some transcendental dogma of his own, as Mr. Moore may possibly have, which mixes man with nature or claims to see other values in men, I shall say no more than that my religion is different from his, and I am uncommonly glad of it. But if he simply says that men cannot be equal because some of them are clever and some of them are stupid—why then I shall merely agree (not without tears) that some of them are very stupid.

G. K. CHESTERTON

THE SENTIMENTALISM OF DIVORCE

Divorce is a thing which the newspapers now not only advertise, but advocate, almost as if it were a pleasure in itself. It may be, indeed, that all the flowers and festivities will now be transferred from the fashionable wedding to the fashionable divorce. A superb iced and frosted divorce-cake will be provided for the feast, and in military circles will be cut with the co-respondent's sword. A dazzling display of divorce presents will be laid out for the inspection of the company, watched by a detective dressed as an ordinary divorce guest. Perhaps the old divorce breakfast will be revived; anyhow, toasts will be drunk, the guests will assemble on the doorstep to see the husband and wife go off in opposite directions; and all will go merry as a divorce-court bell. All this, though to some it might seem a little fanciful, would really be far less fantastic than the sort of things that are really said on the subject. I am not going to discuss the depth and substance of that subject. I myself hold a mystical view of marriage; but I am not going to debate it here. But merely in the interests of light and logic I would protest against the way in which it is frequently debated. The process cannot rationally be called a debate at all. It is a sort of chorus of sentimentalists in the sensational newspapers, perpetually intoning some such formula as this: "We respect marriage, we reverence marriage, holy, sacred, ineffably exquisite and ideal marriage. True marriage is love, and when love alters, marriage alters, and when love stops or begins again, marriage does the same; wonderful, beautiful, beatific marriage."

Now, with all reasonable sympathy with everything sentimental, I may remark that all that talk is tosh. Marriage is an institution like any other, set up deliberately to have certain functions and limitations; it is an institution like private property, or conscription, or the legal liberties of the subject. To talk as if it were made or melted with certain changing moods is a mere waste of words. The object of private property is that as many citizens as possible should have a certain dignity and pleasure in being masters of material things. But suppose a dog-stealer were to say that as soon as a man was bored with his dog it ceased to be his dog, and he ceased to be responsible for it. Suppose he were to say that by merely coveting the dog, he could immediately morally possess the dog. The answer would be that the only way to make men responsible for dogs was to make the relation a legal one, apart from the likes and dislikes of the moment. Suppose a burglar were to say: "Private property I venerate, private property I revere; but I am convinced that Mr. Brown does not truly value his silver Apostle spoons as such sacred objects should be valued; they have therefore ceased to be his property; in reality they have already become my property, for I appreciate their precious character

G. K. CHESTERTON

as nobody else can do." Suppose a murderer were to say: "What can be more amiable and admirable than human life lived with a due sense of its priceless opportunity! But I regret to observe that Mr. Robinson has lately been looking decidedly tired and melancholy; life accepted in this depressing and demoralizing spirit can no longer truly be called life; it is rather my own exuberant and perhaps exaggerated joy of life which I must gratify by cutting his throat with a carving-knife."

It is obvious that these philosophers would fail to understand what we mean by a rule, quite apart from the problem of its exceptions. They would fail to grasp what we mean by an institution, whether it be the institution of law, of property, or of marriage. A reasonable person will certainly reply to the burglar: "You will hardly soothe us by merely poetical praises of property; because your case would be much more convincing if you denied, as the Communists do, that property ought to exist at all. There may be, there certainly are, gross abuses in private property; but, so long as it is an institution at all, it cannot alter merely with moods and emotions. A farm cannot simply float away from a farmer, in proportion as his interest in it grows fainter than it was. A house cannot shift away by inches from a householder, by certain fine shades of feeling that he happens to have about it. A dog cannot drift away like a dream, and begin to belong to somebody else who happens just then to be dreaming of him. And neither can the serious social relation of husband and wife, of mother and father, or even of man and woman, be resolved in all its relations by passions and reactions of sentiment." This question is quite apart from the question of whether there are exceptions to the rule of loyalty, or what they are. The primary point is that there is an institution to which to be loyal. If the new sentimentalists mean what they say, when they say they venerate that institution, they must not suggest that an institution can be actually identical with an emotion. And that is what their rhetoric does suggest, so far as it can be said to suggest anything.

These writers are always explaining to us why they believe in divorce. I think I can easily understand why they believe in divorce. What I do not understand is why they believe in marriage. Just as the philosophical burglar would be more philosophical if he were a Bolshevist, so this sort of divorce advocate would be more philosophical if he were a free-lover. For his arguments never seem to touch on marriage as an institution, or anything more than an individual experience. The real explanation of this strange indifference to the institutional idea is, I fancy, something not only deeper, but wider; something affecting all the institutions of the modern world. The truth is that these sociologists are not at all interested in promoting the sort of social life that marriage does promote. The sort of society of which marriage has always been the strongest pillar is what is sometimes called the distributive society;

the society in which most of the citizens have a tolerable share of property, especially property in land. Everywhere, all over the world, the farm goes with the family and the family with the farm. Unless the whole domestic group hold together with a sort of loyalty or local patriotism, unless the inheritance of property is logical and legitimate, unless the family quarrels are kept out of the courts of officialism, the tradition of family ownership cannot be handed on unimpaired. On the other hand, the Servile State, which is the opposite of the distributive state, has always been rather embarrassed by the institution of marriage. It is an old story that the negro slavery of "Uncle Tom's Cabin" did its worst work in the breaking-up of families. But, curiously enough, the same story is told from both sides. For the apologists of the Slave States, or, at least, of the Southern States, made the same admission even in their own defence. If they denied breaking up the slave family, it was because they denied that there was any slave family to break up.

Free love is the direct enemy of freedom. It is the most obvious of all the bribes that can be offered by slavery. In servile societies a vast amount of sexual laxity can go on in practice, and even in theory, save when now and then some cranky speculator or crazy squire has a fad for some special breed of slaves like a breed of cattle. And even that lunacy would not last long; for lunatics are the minority among slave-owners. Slavery has a much more sane and a much more subtle appeal to human nature than that. It is much more likely that, after a few such fads and freaks, the new Servile State would settle down into the sleepy resignation of the old Servile State; the old pagan repose in slavery, as it was before Christianity came to trouble and perplex the world with ideals of liberty and chivalry. One of the conveniences of that pagan world is that, below a certain level of society, nobody really need bother about pedigree or paternity at all. A new world began when slaves began to stand on their dignity as virgin martyrs. Christendom is the civilization that such martyrs made; and slavery is its returning enemy. But of all the bribes that the old pagan slavery can offer, this luxury and laxity is the strongest; nor do I deny that the influences desiring the degradation of human dignity have here chosen their instrument well.

G. K. CHESTERTON

STREET CRIES AND
STRETCHING THE LAW

About a hundred years ago some enemy sowed among our people the heresy that it is more practical to use a corkscrew to open a sardine-tin, or to employ a door-scraper as a paperweight. Practical politics came to mean the habit of using everything for some other purpose than its own; of snatching up anything as a substitute for something else. A law that had been meant to do one thing, and had conspicuously failed to do it, was always excused because it might do something totally different and perhaps directly contrary. A custom that was supposed to keep everything white was allowed to survive on condition that it made everything black. In reality this is so far from being practical that it does not even rise to the dignity of being lazy. At the best it can only claim to save trouble, and it does not even do that. What it really means is that some people will take every other kind of trouble in the world, if they are saved the trouble of thinking. They will sit for hours trying to open a tin with a corkscrew, rather than make the mental effort of pursuing the abstract, academic, logical connexion between a corkscrew and a cork.

Here is an example of the sort of thing I mean, which I came across in a daily paper to-day. A head-line announces in staring letters, and with startled notes of exclamation, that some abominable judicial authority has made the monstrous decision that musicians playing in the street are not beggars. The journalist bitterly remarks that they may shove their hats under our very noses for money, but yet we must not call them beggars. He follows this remark with several notes of exclamation, and I feel inclined to add a few of my own. The most astonishing thing about the matter, to my mind, is that the journalist is quite innocent in his own indignation. It never so much as crosses his mind that organ-grinders are not classed as beggars because they are not beggars. They may be as much of a nuisance as beggars; they may demand special legislation like beggars; it may be right and proper for every philanthropist to stop them, starve them, harry them, and hound them to death just as if they were beggars. But they are not beggars, by any possible definition of begging. Nobody can be said to be a mere mendicant who is offering something in exchange for money, especially if it is something which some people like and are willing to pay for. A street singer is no more of a mendicant than Madame Clara Butt, though the method (and the scale) of remuneration differs more or less. Anybody who sells anything, in the streets or in the shops, is begging in the sense of begging people to buy. Mr. Selfridge is begging people to buy; the Imperial International Universal Cosmic Stores is begging people to buy. The only possible definition of the actual beggar is not that he is begging people to buy, but that he has nothing to sell.

Now, it is interesting to ask ourselves what the

newspaper really meant, when it was so wildly il-logical in what it said. Superficially and as a mat-ter of mood or feeling, we can all guess what was meant. The writer meant that street musicians looked very much like beggars, because they wore thinner and dirtier clothes than his own; and that he had grown quite used to people who looked like that being treated anyhow and arrested for everything. That is a state of mind not uncommon among those whom economic security has kept as superficial as a varnish. But what was intellectually involved in his vague argument was more interesting. What he meant was, in that deeper sense, that it would be a great convenience if the law that punishes beggars could be *stretched* to cover people who are certainly not beggars, but who may be as much of a bother-ation as beggars. In other words, he wanted to use the mendicity laws in a matter quite unconnected with mendicity; but he wanted to use the old laws because it would save the trouble of making new laws—as the corkscrew would save the trouble of go-ing to look for the tin-opener. And for this notion of the crooked and anomalous use of laws, for ends log-ically different from their own, he could, of course, find much support in the various sophists who have attacked reason in recent times. But, as I have said, it does not really save trouble; and it is becoming increasingly doubtful whether it will even save di-saster. It used to be said that this rough-and-ready method made the country richer; but it will be found less and less consoling to explain why the country is richer when the country is steadily growing poorer. It will not comfort us in the hour of failure to listen to long and ingenious explanations of our success. The truth is that this sort of practical compromise has not led to practical success. The success of England came as the culmination of the highly logical and theoretical eighteenth century. The method was already beginning to fail by the time we came to the end of the compromising and constitutional nineteenth century. Modern scientific civilization was launched by logicians. It was only wrecked by practical men. Anyhow, by this time everybody in England has given up pretending to be particularly rich. It is, therefore, no appropriate moment for proving that a course of being consistently unreasonable will always lead to riches.

In truth, it would be much more practical to be more logical. If street musicians are a nuisance, let them be legislated against for being a nuisance. If begging is really wrong, a logical law should be imposed on all beggars, and not merely on those whom particular persons happen to regard as being also nuisances. What this sort of opportunism does is simply to prevent any question being considered as a whole. I happen to think the whole modern attitude towards beggars is entirely heathen and inhuman. I should be prepared to maintain, as a matter of general morality, that it is intrinsically indefensible to punish human beings for asking for human

G. K. CHESTERTON

assistance. I should say that it is intrinsically insane to urge people to give charity and forbid people to accept charity. Nobody is penalized for crying for help when he is drowning; why should he be penalized for crying for help when he is starving? Every one would expect to have to help a man to save his life in a shipwreck; why not a man who has suffered a shipwreck of his life? A man may be in such a position by no conceivable fault of his own; but in any case his fault is never urged against him in the parallel cases. A man is saved from shipwreck without inquiry about whether he has blundered in the steering of his ship; and we fish him out of a pond before asking whose fault it was that he fell into it. A striking social satire might be written about a man who was rescued again and again out of mere motives of humanity in all the wildest places of the world; who was heroically rescued from a lion and skilfully saved out of a sinking ship; who was sought out on a desert island and scientifically recovered from a deadly swoon; and who only found himself suddenly deserted by all humanity when he reached the city that was his home.

In the ultimate sense, therefore, I do not myself disapprove of mendicants. Nor do I disapprove of musicians. It may not unfairly be retorted that this is because I am not a musician. I allow full weight to the fairness of the retort, but I cannot think it a good thing that even musicians should lose all their feelings except the feeling for music. And it may surely be said that a man must have lost most of his feelings if he does not feel the pathos of a barrel-organ in a poor street. But there are other feelings besides pathos covered by any comprehensive veto upon street music and minstrelsy. There are feelings of history, and even of patriotism. I have seen in certain rich and respectable quarters of London a notice saying that all street cries are forbidden. If there were a notice up to say that all old tombstones should be carted away like lumber, it would be rather less of an act of vandalism. Some of the old street cries of London are among the last links that we have with the London of Shakespeare and the London of Chaucer. When I meet a man who utters one I am so far from regarding him as a beggar; it is I who should be a beggar, and beg him to say it again.

But in any case it should be made clear that we cannot make one law do the work of another. If we have real reasons for forbidding something like a street cry, we should give the reasons that are real; we should forbid it because it is a cry, because it is a noise, because it is a nuisance, or perhaps, according to our tastes, because it is old, because it is popular, because it is historic and a memory of Merry England. I suspect that the subconscious prejudice against it is rooted in the fact that the pedlar or hawker is one of the few free men left in the modern city; that he often sells his own wares directly to the consumer, and does not pay rent for a shop. But if the modern spirit wishes to veto him, to harry him, or to hang,

G. K. CHESTERTON

draw and quarter him for being free, at least let it so far recognize his dignity as to define him; and let the law deal with him in principle as well as in practice.

THE REVOLT OF THE SPOILT CHILD

Everybody says that each generation revolts against the last. Nobody seems to notice that it generally revolts against the revolt of the last. I mean that the latest grievance is really the last reform. To take but one example in passing. There is a new kind of novel which I have seen widely reviewed in the newspapers. No; it is not an improper novel. On the contrary, it is more proper—almost in the sense of prim—than its authors probably imagine. It is really a reaction towards a more old-fashioned morality, and away from a new-fashioned one. It is not so much a revolt of the daughters as a return of the grandmothers.

Miss May Sinclair wrote a novel of the kind I mean, about a spinster whose life had been blighted by a tender and sensitive touch in her education, which had taught her—or rather, expected her—always to "behave beautifully." Mrs. Delafield wrote a story with the refreshing name of "Humbug" on somewhat similar lines. It suggests that children are actually trained to deception, and especially self-deception, by a delicate and considerate treatment that continually appealed to their better feelings, which was always saying, "You would not hurt father." Now, certainly a more old-fashioned and simple style of education did not invariably say "You would not hurt father." Sometimes it preferred to say, "Father will hurt you."

I am not arguing for or against the father with the big stick. I am pointing out that Miss Sinclair and the modern novelists really *are* arguing for the father with the big stick, and against a more recent movement that is supposed to have reformed him. I myself can remember the time when the progressives offered us, as a happy prospect, the very educational method which the novelists now describe so bitterly in retrospect. We were told that true education would only appeal to the better feelings of children; that it would devote itself entirely to telling them to live beautifully; that it would use no argument more arbitrary than saying "You would not hurt father." That ethical education was the whole plan for the rising generation in the days of my youth. We were assured beforehand how much more effective such a psychological treatment would be than the bullying and blundering idea of authority. The hope of the future was in this humanitarian optimism in the training of the young; in other words, the hope was set on something which, when it is established, Mrs. Delafield instantly calls humbug and Miss Sinclair appears to hate as a sort of hell. What they are suffering from, apparently, is not the abuses of their grandfathers, but the most modern reforms of their fathers. These complaints are the first fruits of reformed education, of ethical societies and social idealists. I repeat that I am for the moment talking about their opinions and not mine. I am not eulogizing either big sticks or psychological scalpels; I am pointing out that the outcry against the scalpel

G. K. CHESTERTON

inevitably involves something of a case for the stick. I have never tied myself to a final belief in either; but I point out that the progressive, generation after generation, does elaborately tie himself up in new knots, and then roar and yell aloud to be untied.

It seems a little hard on the late Victorian idealist to be so bitterly abused merely for being kind to his children. There is something a little unconsciously comic about the latest generation of critics, who are crying out against their parents, "Never, never can I forgive the tenderness with which my mother treated me." There is a certain irony in the bitterness which says, "My soul cries for vengeance when I remember that papa was always polite at the breakfast-table; my soul is seared by the persistent insolence of Uncle William in refraining from clouting me over the head." It seems harsh to blame these idealists for idealizing human life, when they were only following what was seriously set before them as the only ideal of education. But, if this is to be said for the late Victorian idealist, there is also something to be said for the early Victorian authoritarian. Upon their own argument, there is something to be said for Uncle William if he did clout them over the head. It is rather hard, even on the great-grandfather with the big stick, that we should still abuse him merely for having neglected the persuasive methods that we have ourselves abandoned. It is hard to revile him for not having discovered to be sound the very sentimentalities that we have since discovered to be rotten.

For the case of these moderns is worst of all when they do try to find any third ideal, which is neither the authority which they once condemned for not being persuasion, nor the persuasion which they now condemn for being worse than authority. The nearest they can get to any other alternative is some notion about individuality; about drawing out the true personality of the child, or allowing a human being to find his real self. It is, perhaps, the most utterly meaningless talk in the whole muddle of the modern world. How is a child of seven to decide whether he has or has not found his true individuality? How, for that matter, is any grown-up person to tell it for him? How is anybody to know whether anybody has become his true self? In the highest sense it can only be a matter of mysticism; it can only mean that there was a purpose in his creation. It can only be the purpose of God, and even then it is a mystery. In anybody who does not accept the purpose of God, it can only be a muddle. It is so unmeaning that it cannot be called mystery but only mystification. Humanly considered, a human personality is only the thing that does in fact emerge out of a combination of the forces inside the child and the forces outside. The child cannot grow up in a void or vacuum with no forces outside. Circumstances will control or contribute to his character, whether they are the grandfather's stick or the father's persuasion or the conversations among the characters of Miss May Sinclair. Who in the world is to say positively

G. K. CHESTERTON

which of these things has or has not helped his real personality?

What is his real personality? These philosophers talk as if there was a complete and complex animal curled up inside every baby, and we had nothing to do but to let it come out with a yell. As a matter of fact, we all know, in the case of the finest and most distinguished personalities, that it would be very difficult to disentangle them from the trials they have suffered, as well as from the truths they have found. But, anyhow, these thinkers must give us some guidance as to how they propose to tell whether their transcendental notion of a true self has been realized or no. As it is, anybody can say of any part of any personality that it is or is not an artificial addition obscuring that personality. In fiction, most of the wild and anarchical characters strike me as entirely artificial. In real life they would no doubt be much the same, if they could ever be met with in real life. But anyhow, they would be the products of experience as well as of elemental impulses; they would be influenced in some way by all they had gone through; and anybody would be free to speculate on what they would have been like if they had never had such experiences. Anybody might amuse himself by trying to subtract the experiences and find the self; anybody who wanted to waste his time.

Therefore, without feeling any fixed fanaticism for all the old methods, whether coercive or persuasive, I do think they both had a basis of common sense which is wanting in this third theory. The parent, whether persuading or punishing the child, was at least aware of one simple truth. He knew that, in the most serious sense, God alone knows what the child is really like, or is meant to be really like. All we can do to him is to fill him with those truths which we believe to be equally true whatever he is like. We must have a code of morals which we believe to be applicable to all children, and impose it on this child because it is applicable to all children. If it seems to be a part of his personality to be a swindler or a torturer, we must tell him that we do not want any personalities to be swindlers and torturers. In other words, we must believe in a religion or philosophy firmly enough to take the responsibility of acting on it, however much the rising generations may knock, or kick, at the door. I know all about the word education meaning drawing things out, and mere instruction meaning putting things in. And I respectfully reply that God alone knows what there is to draw out; but we can be reasonably responsible for what we are ourselves putting in.

G. K. CHESTERTON

THE INNOCENCE OF THE CRIMINAL

A phrase, which we have all heard, is sometimes uttered by some small man sentenced to some small term of imprisonment, for either or both of the two principal reasons for imprisoning a man in modern England: that he is known to the police, and that he is not known to the magistrate. When such a man receives a more or less temperate term of imprisonment, he is often reported as having left the dock saying that he would "do it on his head." In his own self-consciousness, he is merely seeking to maintain his equilibrium by that dazed and helpless hilarity which is the only philosophy allowed to him. But the phrase itself, like a great part of really popular slang, is highly symbolic. The English pauper (who tends to become numerically the preponderant Englishman) does really reconcile himself to existence by putting himself in an inverted and grotesque posture towards it. He does really stand on his head, because he is living in topsy-turvydom.

He finds himself in an Upsidonia fully as fantastic as Mr. Archibald Marshall's, and far less fair and logical; in a landscape as wild as if the trees grew downwards or the moon hung below his feet. He lives in a world in which the man who lends him money makes him a beggar; in which, when he is a beggar, the man who gives him money makes him a criminal; in which, when he is a criminal and "known to the police," he becomes permanently liable to be arrested for other people's crimes. He is punished if his home is neglected, though there is nobody to look after it, and punished again if it is not neglected, and the children are kept from school to look after it. He is arrested for sleeping on private land, and arrested again for sleeping on public land, and arrested, be it noted, for the positive and explicit reason that he has no money to sleep anywhere else. In short, he is under laws of such naked and admitted lunacy that they might quite as well tell him to pluck all the feathers off the cows, or to amputate the left leg of a whale. There is no possible way of behaving in such a pantomime city except as a sort of comic acrobat, a knockabout comedian who does as many things as possible on his head. He is, both by accident and design, a tumbler. It is a proverb about his children that they tumble up; it is the whole joke about his drunkenness that he tumbles down. But he is in a world in which standing straight or standing still have become both impossible and fatal. Meredith rightly conceived the only possible philosophy of this modern outlaw as that of Juggling Jerry; and even what is called his swindling is mostly this sort of almost automatic juggling. His nearest approach to social status is mere kinetic stability, like a top. There was, indeed, another tumbler called in tradition Our Lady's Tumbler, who performed happier antics before a shrine in the days of superstition; and whose philosophy was perhaps more positive than Juggling Jerry's or Meredith's. But a strenuous reform has passed through our own cities, careful of the survival of the fittest, and we have been able to preserve the antic while abolishing the altar.

But though this form of reaction into ridicule, and even self-ridicule, is very natural, it is also very national; it is not the only human reaction against injustice, nor perhaps the most obvious. The Irishman has shot his landlord, the Italian has joined a revolutionary secret society, the Russian has either thrown a bomb or gone on a pilgrimage, long before the Englishman has come finally to the conclusion that existence is a joke. Even as he does so he is too fully conscious that it would be too bad as a tragedy if it were not so good as a farce. It is further to be noticed, for the fact is of ominous importance, that this topsy-turvy English humour has, during the last six or seven generations, been more and more abandoned to the poorer orders. Sir John Falstaff is a knight; Tony Weller is a coachman; his son Sam is a servant to the middle classes, and the recent developments of social discipline seem calculated to force Sam Weller into the status of the Artful Dodger. It is certain that a youth of that class who should do to-day a tenth of the things that Sam Weller did would in one way or another spend most of his life in jail. To-day, indeed, it is the main object of social reform that he should spend the whole of his life in jail; but in a jail that can be used as a factory. That is the real meaning of all the talk about scientific criminology and remedial penalties. For such outcasts, punishment is to be abolished by being perpetuated. When men propose to eliminate retribution as "vindictive," they mean two very simple things: ceasing altogether to punish the few who are rich, and enslaving all the rest for being poor.

Nevertheless this half-conscious buffoon who is the butt of our society is also the satirist of it. He is even the judge of it, in the sense that he is the normal test by which it will be judged. In a number of quite practical matters it is he who represents historic humanity, and speaks naturally and truthfully where his judges and critics are crooked, crabbed and superstitious. This can be seen, for instance, if we see him for a moment not in the dock but in the witness-box. In several books and newspapers I happened to read lately, I have noticed a certain tone touching the uneducated witness; phrases like "the vagueness characteristic of their class," or "easily confused, as such witnesses are." Now such vagueness is simple truthfulness. Nine times out of ten, it is the confusion any man would show at any given instant about the complications which crowd human life. Nine times out of ten, it is avoided in the case of educated witnesses by the mere expedient of a legal fiction. The witness has a brief, like the barrister: he has consulted dates, he has made memoranda, he has frequently settled with solicitors exactly what he can safely say. His evidence is artificial even when it

G. K. CHESTERTON

is not fictitious; we might almost say it is fictitious even when it is not false. The model testimony, regarded as the most regular of all in a law court, is constabulary testimony; if what the soldier said is not evidence, what the policeman says is often the only evidence. And what the policeman says is incredible, as he says it. It is something like this: "I met the prisoner coming out of Clapham Junction Station and he told me he went to see Mrs. Nehemiah Blagg, of 192, Paardeburg Terrace, West Ealing, about a cat which he had left there last Tuesday week which she was going to keep if it was a good mouser, and she told him it had killed a mouse in the back kitchen on Sunday morning so he had better leave it. She gave him a shilling for his trouble, and he went to West Ealing post-office where he bought two halfpenny stamps and a ball of string, and then to the Imperial Stores at Ealing Broadway, and bought a pennyworth of mixed sweets. Coming out he met a friend, and they went to the Green Dolphin and made an appointment for 5.30 next day at the third lamp-post in Eckstein Street," and so on. It is frankly impossible for anybody to say such a sentence; still more for anybody to remember it. If the thing is not a tissue of mere inventions, it can only be the arbitrary summary of a very arbitrary cross-examination, conducted precisely as are the examinations of a secret police in Russia. The story was not only discovered bit by bit, but discovered backwards. Mountains were in labour to bring forth that mouse in West Ealing. The police made a thorough official search of the man's mental boxes and baggage, before that cat was let out of the bag. I am not here supposing the tale to be untrue—I am pointing out that the telling of it is unreal. The right way to tell a story is the way in which the prisoner told it to the policeman, and not the way in which the policeman tells it to the court. It is the way in which all true tales are told, the way in which all men learn the news about their neighbours, the way in which we all learned everything we know in childhood; it is the only real evidence for anything on this earth, and it is not evidence in a court of law. The man who tells it is vague about some things, less vague about others, and so on in proportion; but at his very vaguest, among the stiff unreason of modern conditions, he is a judgment on those conditions. His very bewilderment is a criticism, and his very indecision is a decision against us. It is an old story that we are judged by the innocence of a child, and every child is, in the French phrase, a terrible child. There is a true sense in which all our laws are judged by the innocence of a criminal.

In politics, of course, the case is the same. I will defer the question of whether the democracy knows how to answer questions until the oligarchy knows how to ask them. Asking a man if he approves of Tariff Reform is not only a silly but an insane question, for it covers the wildest possibilities, just as asking him whether he approves of Trouser Reform might mean anything from wearing no trousers to wearing

G. K. CHESTERTON

a particular pattern of yellow trousers decorated with scarlet snakes. Talking about Temperance, when you mean pouring wine down the gutter, is quite literally as senseless as talking about Thrift, when you mean throwing money into the sea. The rambling speech of yokels and tramps is as much wiser than this as a rambling walk in the woods is wiser than the mathematical straightness of a fall from a precipice. The present leaders of progress are, I think, very near to that precipice; about all their schemes and ideals there is a savour of suicide. But the clown will go on talking in a living and, therefore, a leisurely fashion, and the great truth of pure gossip which sprang up in simpler ages and was the fountain of all the literatures, will flow on when our intricate and tortured society has died of its sins.

THE PRUDERY OF THE FEMINISTS

In the ultimate and universal sense I am astonished at the lack of astonishment. Starting from scratch, so to speak, we are all in the position of the first frog, whose pious and compact prayer was: "Lord, how you made me jump!" Matthew Arnold told us to see life steadily and see it whole. But the flaw in his whole philosophy is that when we do see life whole we do not see it steadily, in Arnold's sense, but as a staggering prodigy of creation. There is a primeval light in which all stones are precious stones; a primeval darkness against which all flowers are as vivid as fireworks. Nevertheless, there is one kind of surprise that does surprise me, the more, perhaps, because it is not true surprise but a supercilious fuss. There is a kind of man who not only claims that his stone is the only pebble on the beach, but declares it must be the one and only philosopher's stone, because he is the one and only philosopher. He does not discover suddenly the sensational fact that grass is green. He discovers it very slowly, and proves it still more slowly, bringing us one blade of grass at a time. He is made haughty instead of humble by hitting on the obvious. The flowers do not make him open his eyes, but, rather, cover them with spectacles; and this is even more true of the weeds and thorns. Even his bad news is banal. A young man told me he had abandoned his

Bible religion and vicarage environment at the with- ering touch of the one line of Fitzgerald: "The flower that once has blown, for ever dies." I vainly pointed out that the Bible or the English burial service could have told him that man cometh up as a flower and is cut down. If that were self-evidently final, there would never have been any Bibles or any vicarages. I do not see how the flower can be any more dead, when a mower can cut it down, merely because a bot- anist can cut it up. It should further be remembered that the belief in the soul, right or wrong, arose and flourished among men who knew all there is to know about cutting down, not unfrequently cutting each other down, with considerable vivacity. The physical fact of death, in a hundred horrid shapes, was more naked and less veiled in times of faith or superstition than in times of science or scepticism. Often it was not merely those who had seen a man die, but those who had seen him rot, who were most certain that he was everlastingly alive.

There is another case somewhat analogous to this discovery of the new disease of death. I am puzzled in somewhat the same way when I hear, as we often hear just now, somebody saying that he was formerly opposed to Female Suffrage but was converted to it by the courage and patriotism shown by women in nursing and similar war work. Really, I do not wish to be superior in my turn, when I can only express my wonder in a question. But from what benighted dens can these people have crawled, that they did not know that women are brave? What horrible sort of women have they known all their lives? Where do they come from? Or, what is a still more apposite question, where do they think they come from? Do they think they fell from the moon, or were really found under cabbage-leaves, or brought over the sea by storks? Do they (as seems more likely) believe they were produced chemically by Mr. Schafer on principles of abiogenesis? Should we any of us be here at all if women were not brave? Are we not all trophies of that war and triumph? Does not every man stand on the earth like a graven statue as the monument of the valour of a woman?

As a matter of fact, it is men much more than women who needed a war to redeem their reputation, and who have redeemed it. There was much more plausibility in the suspicion that the old torture of blood and iron would prove too much for a somewhat drugged and materialistic male population long estranged from it. I have always suspected that this doubt about manhood was the real sting in the strange sex quarrel, and the meaning of the new and nervous tattoo about the unhappiness of women. Man, like the Master Builder, was suspected by the female intelligence of having lost his nerve for climbing that dizzy battle-tower he had built in times gone by. In this the war did certainly straighten out the sex tangle; but it did also make clear on how terrible a thread of tenure we hold our privileges—and even our pleasures. For even bridge parties and champagne suppers take place on the top of that toppling war-tower; an hour can come when even a man who cared for nothing but bridge would have to defend it like Horatius; or when the man who only lives for champagne would have to die for champagne, as certainly as thousands of French soldiers have died for that flat land of vines; when he would have to fight as hard for the wine as Jeanne D'Arc for the oil of Rheims.

Just as civilization is guarded by potential war, so it is guarded by potential revolution. We ought never to indulge in either without extreme provocation; but we ought to be cured for ever of the fancy that extreme provocation is impossible. Against the tyrant within, as against the barbarian without, every voter should be a potential volunteer. "Thou goest with women, forget not thy whip," said the Prussian philosopher; and some such echo probably infected those who wanted a war to make them respect their wives and mothers. But there would really be a symbolic sense in saying, "Thou goest with men, forget not thy sword." Men coming to the council of the tribe should sheathe their swords, but not surrender them. Now I am not going to talk about Female Suffrage at this time of day; but these were the elements upon which a fair and sane opposition to it were founded. These are the risks of real politics; and the woman was not called upon to run such a risk, for the very simple reason that she was already running another risk. It was not laws that fixed her in the family; it was the very nature of the family. If the family was a fact in any very full sense, and if popular rule was also a fact in any very full sense, it was simply physically impossible for the woman to play the same part in such politics as the man. The difficulty was only evaded because the democracy was not a free democracy or the family not a free family. But whether this view was right or wrong, it is at least clear that the only honourable basis for any limitations of womanhood is the same as the basis of the respect for womanhood. It consisted in certain realities, which it may be undesirable to discuss, but is certainly even more undesirable to ignore. And my complaint against the more fussy feminists (so called from their detestation of everything feminine) is that they do ignore these realities. I do not even propose the alternative of discussing them; on that point I am myself content to be what some call conventional, and others, civilized. I do not in the least demand that anyone should accept my own deduction from them; and I do not care a brass farthing what deduction anybody accepts about such a rag as a modern ballot-paper. But I do suggest that the peril with which one half of humanity is perpetually at war should be at least present in the minds of those who are perpetually bragging about breaking conventions, rending veils, and violating antiquated taboos. And, in nine cases out of ten, it seems to be quite absent from their minds. The mere fact of using the argument before mentioned, of woman's strength vindicated by war work, shows that it is absent from their minds.

If this oddity of the new obscurantism means, rather, that women have shown the moral courage and mental capacity needed for important concerns, I am equally unable to summon up any surprise at the revelation. Nothing can well be more important than our own souls and bodies; and they, at their most delicate and determining period, are almost always and almost entirely confided to women. Those who have been appointed as educational experts in every age are not surely a new order of priestesses. If it means that in a historic crisis all kinds of people must do all kinds of work, and that women are the more to be admired for doing work to which they are unaccustomed, or even unsuited, it is a point which I should quite as warmly concede. But if it means that in planning the foundations of a future society we should ignore the one eternal and incurable contrast in humanity; if it means that we may now go ahead gaily as if there were really no difference at all; if it means, as I read in a magazine to-day, and as almost anyone may now read almost anywhere, that if such and such work is bad for women it must be bad for men; if it means that patriotic women in munition factories prove that any women can be happy in any factories; if, in short, it means that the huge and primeval facts of the family no longer block the way to a mere social assimilation and regimentation—then I say that the prospect is not one of liberty but of perpetuation of the dreariest sort of humbug. It is not emancipation, it is not even anarchy; it is simply

G. K. CHESTERTON

prudery in the thoughts. It means that we have Bowdlerized our brains as well as our books. It is every bit as senseless a surrender to a superstitious decorum as it would be to force every woman to cut herself with a razor, because it is not etiquette to admit that she cannot grow a beard.

HOW MAD LAWS ARE MADE

Any one of the strange laws we suffer is a compromise between a fad and a vested interest. The fashionable way of effecting a social reform is as follows. To make the story clearer, and worthier of its wild and pointless process, I will call the two chief agents in it the March Hare and the Hatter. The Hatter is mad, in a quiet way; but he is merely mad on making hats, or rather on making money. He has a huge and prosperous emporium which advertises all possible hats to fit all possible heads; but he certainly nourishes an occult conviction that it is really the duty of the heads to fit the hats. This is his mild madness; in other respects he is a stodgy and rather stupid millionaire. Now, the man whom we will call the March Hare is at first sight the flat contrary of this. He is a wild intellectual and the leader of the Hatless Brigade. It does not much matter why there is this quarrel between the Hare and the Hat; it may be any progressive sophistry. Perhaps it is because he is a March Hare; and finds it hard to keep his hat on in a March wind. Perhaps it is because his ears are too long to allow him to wear a hat; or perhaps he hopes that every emancipated member of the Hatless Brigade will eventually evolve ears as long as a hare's—or a donkey's. The point is that anyone would fancy that the Hare and the Hatter would collide.

As a matter of fact they co-operate. In other words, every "reform" to-day is a treaty between the two most influential modern figures—the great capitalist and the small faddist. They are the father and mother of a new law; and therefore it is so much of a mongrel as to be a monster.

What happens is something like this. The line of least resistance is found between the two by a more subtle analysis of their real respective aims. The intuitive eye of friendship detects a fine shade in the feelings of the Hatter. The desire of his heart, when delicately apprehended, is not necessarily that people should wear his hats, but rather that they should buy them. On the other hand, even his fanatically consistent colleague has no particular objection to a human being purchasing a hat, so long as he does not wreck his health, blast his prospects and generally blow his brains out, by the one suicidal act of putting it on. Between them they construct a law called the Habitual Hat-Pegs Act, which lays it down that every householder shall have not less than twenty-three hat-pegs and that, lest these should accumulate unwholesome dust, each must be covered by a hat in uninterrupted occupation. Or the thing might be managed some other way; as by arranging that a great modern nobleman should wear an accumulation of hats, one on top of the other, in pleasing memory of what has often been the itinerant occupation of his youth. Broadly, it would be enacted that hats might be used in various ways; to take rabbits out of,

G. K. CHESTERTON

as in the case of conjurers, or put pennies into, as in the case of beggars, or smash on the heads of scarecrows, or stick on the tops of poles; if only it were guaranteed that as many citizens as possible should be forced to go bareheaded. Thus, the two most powerful elements in the governing class are satisfied; of which the first is finance and the second fidgets. The Capitalist has made money; and he only wanted to make money. The Social Reformer has done something; and he only wanted something to do.

Now every one of the recent tricks about temperance and economy has been literally of this type. I have chosen the names from a nonsense story merely for algebraic lucidity and universality; what has really happened in our own shops and streets is every bit as nonsensical. But quite recent events have confirmed this analysis with an accuracy which even the unconverted can hardly regard as a coincidence. I have already traced the truth in the case of the liquor traffic; but many public-spirited persons of the Prohibitionist school have found it very difficult to believe. All "temperance legislation" is a compromise between a liquor merchant who wants to get rid of his liquor and a teetotaller who does not want his neighbours to get it. But as the capitalist is much stronger than the crank, the compromise is lop-sided as such; the neighbours do get it, but always in the wrong way. But again, since the crank has not a true creed, but only an intellectual itch, he cares much more to be up and doing than to understand what he has done. As I said above, he only wants to do something; and he has done something; he has increased drunkenness. Anyhow, all such reforms are upon the plan of my parable. Sometimes it is decreed that drink shall only be sold in large quantities suitable to large incomes; that is exactly like allowing one nobleman to wear twenty hats. Sometimes it is proposed that the State should take over the liquor traffic; we hardly need to be told what that means, when it is the Plutocratic State. It means quite simply this: the policeman goes to the hatter and buys his whole stock of hats at a hundred pounds a piece, and then parades the street handing out hats to those who may take his fancy, and by blows of the truncheon forcing every man Jack of the rest of them to pay a hundred pounds for a hat he does not get. Merely to divert the rivers of ale or gin from private power to public power or from poor men to rich men, or from good taverns to bad taverns, is the sort of effort with which the faddists are satisfied and the liquor lords much more than satisfied.

There was a curious case of the same thing in the attempt to economize food during the Great War. The reformers did not wish *really* to economize food; the great food profiteers would not let them. The fussy person wants to force or forbid something, under the conditions defining all such effort; it must be something that will interfere with the citizen and will not interfere with the profiteer. Given such a problem, we might almost predict, for instance, that he will

G. K. CHESTERTON

propose the limitation of the number of courses at a restaurant. It will not save the beef; it is not meant to save the beef; but to save the beef-merchant. There will actually be more food bought, if the cook is not allowed to turn the scraps into kickshaws. But why should a plutocracy including food profiteers object to more food being bought? Why, for that matter, should the pure-minded social idealist object to more food being bought, as long as it is the wrong food that is sold? His quite disinterested aim is not that food should be restricted, but merely that freedom should be restricted. When once he is assured that a sufficient number of thoughtless persons are really getting what they don't want, he says he is building Jerusalem in England's green and pleasant land. And so he is; if the expression signifies handing over England to the wealthier Jews.

Now the only way in which this conclusive explanation can be countered is by ridiculing, as impossible, the notion that so fantastic a compact can be clearly and coolly made. And of course it is not so made. The two attitudes are not logically interlocked, like the antlers of stags; they simply squeeze each other out of shape, as in a wrestle of two rival jelly-fish. We should be far safer if they had the intellectual honesty of a bargain or a bribe. As it is, they have an almost creepy quality which justifies the comparison to shapeless beasts of the sea. I defy any rational man to deny that he has noticed something moonstruck and mis-shapen, as apart from anything unjust or

uncomfortable, about the little laws which have lately been tripping him up; laws which may tell him
at any minute that he must not purchase turpentine
before a certain tick of the clock, or that if he buys
a pound of tea he must also buy a pennyworth of
tin-tacks. The strictly correct word for such things is
half-witted; and they are half-witted because each of
the two incongruous partners has only half his will.
They have not, for instance, the sweeping simplicity
of the old sumptuary laws or even the old Puritan
persecutions. But they are also half-witted because
even the one mind is not the whole mind; it is largely
the subconscious mind, which dares not trust itself in
speech. The Drink Capitalist dares not actually say
to the teetotaller, "Let me sell a quart bottle of whis-
ky to be drunk in a day, and then I will let you pester
a poor fellow who makes a pot of beer last half an
hour." That is exactly what happens in essence; but it
is easy to guess what happens in external form. The
teetotaller has twenty schemes for cutting off free
citizens from the beverage of their fathers; and out
of these twenty the liquor lord, without whose permission nothing can be done, selects the one scheme
which will not interfere with him and his money. It
is even more probable that the temperance reformer
himself selects, by an instinct for what he would call
practical politics, the one scheme which the liquor
lord is likely to look at. And it matters nothing that it
is a scheme too witless for Wonderland; a scheme for
abolishing hats while preserving hatters.

G. K. CHESTERTON

It might be a good thing to give the control of drink to the State—if there were a State to give it to. But there is not. There is nothing but a congested compromise made by the pressure of powerful interests on each other. The liquor lords may bargain with the other lords to take their abnormal tribute in a lump instead of a lifetime; but not one of them will live the poorer. The main point is that, in passing through that plutocratic machinery, even a mad opinion will always emerge in a shape more maniacal than its own; and even the silliest fool can only do what the stupidest fool will let him.

THE PAGODA OF PROGRESS

There is one fashionable fallacy that crops up everywhere like a weed, until a man feels inclined to devote the rest of his life to the hopeless task of weeding it out. I take one example of it from a newspaper correspondence headed "Have Women Gone Far Enough?" It is immediately concerned with alleged impropriety in dress; but I am not directly interested in that. I quote one paragraph from a lady correspondent, not because it is any worse than the same thing as stated by countless scholars and thinkers, but rather because it is more clearly stated—

"'Women have gone far enough.' That has always been the cry of the individual with the unprogressive mind. It seems to me that until Doomsday there will always be the type of man who will cry 'Women have gone far enough'; but no one can stop the tide of evolution, and women will still go on."

Which raises the interesting question of where they will go to. Now, as a matter of fact, every thinking person wants to stop the tide of evolution at some particular mark in his own mind. If I were to propose that people should wear no clothes at all, the lady might be shocked. But I should have as much right as anyone else to say that she was obviously an individual with an unprogressive mind. If I were to propose that this reform should be imposed on people by force, she would be justly indignant. But I could answer her with her own argument—that there had always been unprogressive people, and would be till Doomsday. If I then proposed that people should not only be stripped but skinned alive, she might, perhaps, see several moral objections. But her own argument would still hold good, or as good as it held in her own case; and I could say that evolution would not stop and the skinning would go on. The argument is quite as good on my side as on hers; and it is worthless on both.

Of course, it would be just as easy to urge people to progress or evolve in exactly the opposite direction. It would be as easy to maintain that they ought to go on wearing more and more clothes. It might be argued that savages wear fewer clothes, that clothes are a mark of civilization, and that the evolution of them will go on. I am highly civilized if I wear ten hats, and more highly civilized if I wear twelve hats. When I have already evolved so far as to put on six pairs of trousers, I must still hail the appearance of the seventh pair of trousers with the joy due to the waving banner of a great reform. When we balance these two lunacies against each other, the central point of sanity is surely apparent. The man who headed his inquiry "Have Women Gone Far Enough?" was at least in a real sense stating the point rightly. The point is that there *is* a "far enough." There is a

G. K. CHESTERTON

point at which something that was once neglected becomes exaggerated; something that is valuable up to that stage becomes undesirable after that stage. It is possible for the human intellect to consider clearly at what stage, or in what condition, it would have enough complication of clothes, or enough simplification of clothes, or enough of any other social element or tendency. It is possible to set a limit to the pagoda of human hats, rising for ever into infinity. It is possible to count the human legs, and, after a brief calculation, allot to them the appropriate number of trousers. There is such a thing as the miscalculation of making hats for a hydra or boots for a centipede, just as there are such things as bare-footed friars or the Hatless Brigade. There are exceptions and exaggerations, good and bad; but the point is that they are not only both good and bad, but they are good and bad in opposite directions. Let a man have what ideal of human costume or custom he likes. That ideal must still consist of elements in a certain proportion; and if that proportion is disturbed that ideal is destroyed. Let him once be clear in his own mind about what he wants, and then, whatever it is that he wants, he will not want the tide of evolution to wash it away. His ideal may be as revolutionary as he likes or as reactionary as he likes, but it must remain as he likes it. To make it more revolutionary or more reactionary is distortion; to suggest its growing more and more reactionary or revolutionary for ever is demented nonsense. How can a man know what he wants, how can he even want what he wants, if it will not even remain the same while he wants it?

The particular argument about women is not primarily the point; but as a matter of fact it is a very good illustration of the point. If a man thinks the Victorian conventions kept women out of things they would be the happier for having, his natural course is to consider what things they are; not to think that any things will do, so long as there are more of them. This is only the sort of living logic everybody acts upon in life. Suppose somebody says, "Don't you think all this wood could be used for something else besides palings?" we shall very probably answer, "Well, I dare say it could," and perhaps begin to think of wooden boxes or wooden stools. But we shall not see, as in a sort of vision, a vista of wooden razors, wooden carving-knives, wooden coats and hats, wooden pillows and pocket-handkerchiefs. If people had made a false and insufficient list of the uses of wood, we shall try to make a true and sufficient list of them; but not imagine that the list can go on for ever, or include more and more of everything in the world. I am not establishing a scientific parallel between wood and womanhood. But there would be nothing disrespectful in the symbol, considered as a symbol; for wood is the most sacred of all substances: it typifies the divine trade of the carpenter, and men count themselves fortunate to touch it. Here it is only a working simile, but the point of it is this—that all this nonsense about progressive and

G. K. CHESTERTON

unprogressive minds, and the tide of evolution, divides people into those who stick ignorantly to wood for one thing and those who attempt insanely to use wood for everything. Both seem to think it a highly eccentric suggestion that we should find out what wood is really useful for, and use it for that. They either profess to worship a wooden womanhood inside the wooden fences of certain trivial and temporary Victorian conventions; or else they profess to see the future as a forest of dryads growing more and more feminine for ever.

But it does not matter to the main question whether anybody else draws the line exactly where I do. The point is that I am not doing an illogical thing, but the only logical thing, in drawing the line. I think tennis for women normal and football for women quite abnormal; and I am no more inconsistent than I am in having a wooden walking-stick and not a wooden hat. I do not particularly object to a female despot; but I do object to a female demagogue. And my distinction is as much founded on the substance of things as my eccentric conduct in having a wooden chair and table but not a wooden knife and fork. You may think my division wrong; the point is that it is not wrong in being a division. All this fallacy of false progress tends to obscure the old common sense of all mankind, which is still the common sense of every man in his own daily dealings: that everything has its place and proportion and proper use, and that it is rational to trust its use and distrust its abuse. Progress, in the good sense, does not consist in looking for a direction in which one can go on indefinitely. For there is no such direction, unless it be in quite transcendental things, like the love of God. It would be far truer to say that true progress consists in looking for the place where we can stop.

G. K. CHESTERTON

THE MYTH OF THE "MAYFLOWER"

Agnosticism, the ancient confession of ignorance, was a singularly sane and healthy thing so far as it went. Unfortunately it has not gone as far as the twentieth century. It has declared in all ages, as a heathen chief declared in the dark ages, that the life of a man is like the flight of a bird across a firelit room, because we know nothing of whence it comes or whither it goes. It would seem natural to apply it not only to man but to mankind. But the moderns do not apply the same principle but the very opposite principle. They specialize in the unknown origins and in the unknown future. They dwell on the pre-historic and on the post-historic or prophetic; and neglect only the historic. They will give a most detailed description of the habits of the bird when he was a sort of pterodactyl only faintly to be traced in a fossil. They will give an equally detailed description of the habits of the bird a hundred years hence, when he shall have turned into a super-bird, or the dove of universal peace. But the bird in the hand is worth far less to them than the two mysterious birds in these two impenetrable bushes. Thus they will publish a portrait with life, letters, and tabletalk of the Missing Link, although he is missing; they will publish a plan and documented history of how the Social Revolution happened, though it has not happened yet. It is the men who are not missing and the revolutions that have happened that they have rather a habit of overlooking. Anyone who has argued, for instance, with the young Jewish intellectuals who are the brain of Bolshevism knows that their whole system turns on the two pivots of the prehistoric and the prophetic. They talk of the Communism of prehistoric ages as if it were a thing like the Crusades in the Middle Ages; not even a probable conjecture but a proved and familiar fact. They will tell you exactly how private property arose in primitive times, just as if they had been there. And then they will take one gigantic leap over all human history, and tell you about the inevitable Communism of the future. Nothing seems to matter unless it is either new enough to be foretold or old enough to be forgotten.

Mr. H. G. Wells has hit off his human habit in the account of a very human character, the American girl who glorifies Stonehenge in his last novel. I do not make Mr. Wells responsible for her opinions, though she is an attractive person and much too good for her Lothario. But she interests me here because she typifies very truly another variation upon this same tendency. To the prehistoric and the post-historic must be added a third thing, which may be called the unhistoric. I mean the bad teaching of real history that such intelligent people so often suffer. She sums up exactly what I mean when she says humorously that Stonehenge has been "kept from her," that Notre Dame is far less important, and that this is the real starting-point of the "Mayflower."

Now the "Mayflower" is a myth. It is an intensely interesting example of a real modern myth. I do not mean of course that the "Mayflower" never sailed, any more than I admit that King Arthur never lived or that Roland never died. I do not mean that the incident had no historic interest, or that the men who figured in it had no heroic qualities; any more than I deny that Charlemagne was a great man because the legend says he was two hundred years old; any more than I deny that the resistance of Roman Britain to the heathen invasion was valiant and valuable, because the legend says that Arthur at Mount Badon killed nine hundred men with his own hand. I mean that there exists in millions of modern minds a traditional image or vision called the "Mayflower," which has far less relation to the real facts than Charlemagne's two hundred years or Arthur's nine hundred corpses. Multitudes of people in England and America, as intelligent and sympathetic as the young lady in Mr. Wells' novel, think of the "Mayflower" as an origin or archetype like the Ark or at least the Argo. Perhaps it would be an exaggeration to say that they think the "Mayflower" discovered America. They do really talk as if the "Mayflower" populated America. Above all, they talk as if the establishment of New England had been the first and formative example of the expansion of England. They believe that English expansion was a Puritan experiment; and that an expansion of Puritan ideas was also the expansion of what have been claimed as English ideas, especially ideas of liberty. The Puritans of New England were champions of religious freedom, seeking to found a newer and freer state beyond the sea, and thus becoming the origin and model of modern democracy. All this betrays a lack of exactitude. It is certainly nearer to exact truth to say that Merlin built the castle at Camelot by magic, or that Roland broke the mountains in pieces with his unbroken sword.

For at least the old fables are faults on the right side. They are symbols of the truth and not of the opposite of the truth. They described Roland as brandishing his unbroken sword against the Moslems, but not in favour of the Moslems. And the New England Puritans would have regarded the establishment of real religious liberty exactly as Roland would have regarded the establishment of the religion of Mahound. The fables described Merlin as building a palace for a king and not a public hall for the London School of Economics. And it would be quite as sensible to read the Fabian politics of Mr. Sidney Webb into the local kingships of the Dark Ages, as to read anything remotely resembling modern liberality into the most savage of all the savage theological frenzies of the seventeenth century. Thus the "Mayflower" is not merely a fable, but is much more false than fables generally are. The revolt of the Puritans against the Stuarts was really a revolt *against* religious toleration. I do not say the Puritans

G. K. CHESTERTON

were never persecuted by their opponents; but I do say, to their great honour and glory, that the Puritans never descended to the hypocrisy of pretending for a moment that they did not mean to persecute their opponents. And in the main their quarrel with the Stuarts was that the Stuarts would not persecute those opponents enough. Not only was it then the Catholics who were proposing toleration, but it was they who had already actually established toleration in the State of Maryland, before the Puritans began to establish the most intolerant sort of intolerance in the State of New England. And if the fable is fabulous touching the emancipation of religion, it is yet more fabulous touching the expansion of empire. That had been started long before either New England or Maryland, by Raleigh who started it in Virginia. Virginia is still perhaps the most English of the states, certainly more English than New England. And it was also the most typical and important of the states, almost up to Lee's last battle in the Wilderness. But I have only taken the "Mayflower" as an example of the general truth; and in a way the truth has its consoling side. Modern men are not allowed to have any history; but at least nothing can prevent men from having legends.

We have thus before us, in a very true and typical modern picture, the two essential parts of modern culture. It consists first of false history and second of fancy history. What the American tourist believed about Plymouth Rock was untrue; what she believed about Stonehenge was only unfounded. The popular story of Primitive Man cannot be proved. The popular story of Puritanism can be disproved. I can fully sympathize with Mr. Wells and his heroine in feeling the imaginative stimulus of mysteries like Stonehenge; but the imagination springs from the mystery; that is, the imagination springs from the ignorance. It is the very greatness of Stonehenge that there is very little of it left. It is its chief feature to be featureless. We are very naturally and rightly moved to mystical emotions about signals from so far away along the path of the past; but part of the poetry lies in our inability really to read the signals. And this is what gives an interest, and even an irony, to the comparison half consciously invoked by the American lady herself when she asked "What's Notre Dame to this?" And the answer that should be given to her is: "Notre Dame, compared to this, is *true*. It is history. It is humanity. It is what has really happened, what we know has really happened, what we know is really happening still. It is the central fact of your own civilization. And it is the thing that has really been kept from you."

Notre Dame is not a myth. Notre Dame is not a theory. Its interest does not spring from ignorance but from knowledge; from a culture complicated with a hundred controversies and revolutions. It is not featureless, but carved into an incredible forest and labyrinth of fascinating features, any one of which we could talk about for days. It is not great

G. K. CHESTERTON

because there is little of it, but great because there is a great deal of it. It is true that though there is a great deal of it, Puritans may not be allowed to see a great deal in it; whether they were those brought over in the "Mayflower" or only those brought up on the "Mayflower." But that is not the fault of Notre Dame; but of the extraordinary evasion by which such people can dodge to right and left of it, taking refuge in things more recent or things more remote. Notre Dame, on its merely human side, is mediæval civilization, and therefore not a fable or a guess but a great solid determining part of modern civilization. It is the whole modern debate about the guilds; for such cathedrals were built by the guilds. It is the whole modern question of religion and irreligion; for we know what religion it stands for, while we really have not a notion what religion Stonehenge stands for. A Druid temple is a ruin, and a Puritan ship by this time may well be called a wreck. But a church is a challenge; and that is why it is not answered.

MUCH TOO MODERN HISTORY

All wise men will agree that history ought to be taught more fully in the form of world history. In that respect at least Mr. Wells gave us an excellent working model. England is meaningless without Europe, more meaningless than England without Empire. But those who would broaden history with human brotherhood too often suffer from a limitation not absent even from Mr. Wells. They exchange the narrowness of a nation for the narrowness of a theory, or even a fad. They think they have a world-wide philosophy because they extend their own narrowness to the whole world. A distinguished professor, who is a member of the League of Nations Union, has been telling an interviewer what he thinks history-books should teach. And it seems to me that, according to his view if correctly reported, the new histories would be rather more prejudiced and limited than the old.

He begins with a small but singular error, which itself shows some lack of the imagination that can see two sides of a question. He says, "Textbooks of history should aim at truth. It should not be possible for one version of the American War of Independence to be taught in American schools, and another in English schools."

Now, in point of fact, the same version of that story is taught both in English and American schools. It is the other version, a very tenable one, that is not allowed to be taught anywhere. No American historian, however American, could be more positive that George III was wrong and George Washington right than all the English historians are. What would show real independence of mind would be to state the case for George III. And there was a very real case for George III. I will not go into it here, but every honest historical student will agree with me. Perhaps the fairest way of putting it is this: that it was not really a case of a government resolved on tyranny, but of a nation resolved on independence. But if we sympathize with national independence, surely there is something to be said for intellectual independence. And the professor is far from being really sympathetic with intellectual independence. He is so far from it that he wants both sides forced to tell the same story, apparently whether they like it or not. As a fact, they do agree; but apparently in any case the professor would coerce them into agreement. And his extraordinary reason for this course is that history should aim at truth.

But suppose I do aim at truth, and sincerely come to the conclusion that North was a patriot and Burke a sophist? How would the professor prevent it being "possible" for me to teach what I think is true? The truth is that it has never occurred to these progressive professors that there could be any view of any question except their own, or what they call their own. For it is only a tradition they have been taught; a tradition as narrow as North's and now nearly as old.

G. K. CHESTERTON

But the professor goes on to say something much more interesting and curious. After saying very truly that the past, the Plantagenet period for instance, should not be made a mere matter of kings and battles, he goes on to say, "What we want to see is the textbook of history and the teaching of it brought more closely into touch with the realities of the modern world—the world of the division of labour between different countries, of the application of science to industry, of the shortening of the spaces of the earth by improvements in transport—and with all that these realities imply."

Now it seems to me obvious that what we want is exactly the opposite. A child can see these realities of the modern world, whether he is taught any history or not. He will see them whether you want him to or not. As he grows up he will learn by experience all about the improvements in transport, its acceleration by Zeppelins and its interruption by submarines. He will realize for himself that the modern world is the world of the division of labour between nations. For he will know that England has been turned into an isolated workshop with hardly food enough for a fortnight, with the potential alternative of surrender or starvation or eating nails. He will by the light of nature know all about the application of science to industry—in war by chemical analyses of poison gas, in peace by bright little pamphlets about phossy jaw. He will know "all that these realities imply," about which also there is very much that might be said.

But even if we consider only the somewhat cheerier products of the division of labour and the application of science to industry, there is quite as little need laboriously to instruct the infant in what he can see for himself. A child has a very pure and poetical love of machinery, a love in which there is nothing in the least evil or materialistic. But it is hardly necessary to devote years to proving to him that motor-cars have been invented, as he can see them going by in the street. It is not necessary to read up in the British Museum the details with which to demonstrate that there are really such things as tube stations or motor-bicycles. The child can see these things everywhere, and the real danger obviously is that he should think they had existed always. The danger is that he should know nothing of humanity, except as it is under these special and sometimes cramping conditions of scientific industry and the division of labour. It is that he should be unable to imagine any civilization without tube stations, whatever its substitutes in the way of temples or trophies of war. It is that he should see man as a sort of cyclist-centaur, inseparable from his motor-bike. In short, the whole danger of historical ignorance is that he may be as limited to his local circumstances as a savage on an island, or a provincial in a decayed town, or a historical professor in the League of Nations Union.

The whole object of history is to enlarge experience by imagination. And this sort of history would enlarge neither imagination nor experience. The whole

G. K. CHESTERTON

object of history is to make us realize that humanity could be great and glorious, under conditions quite different and even contrary to our own. It is to teach us that men could achieve most profitable labour without our own division of labour. It is to teach us that men could be industrious without being industrial. It is to make us understand that there might be a world in which there was far less improvement in the transport for visiting various places, and there might still be a very great improvement in the places visited.

The professor is perfectly right in saying that a history of the Plantagenet period ought not merely to record the presence of kings and armies. But what ought it to record? Is it to record only the absence of motors and electric lights? Should we say nothing of the Plantagenet period except that it did *not* have motor-bikes? I venture to suggest that we might record the presence of some things which the whole people had then and have not got now, such as the guilds, the great popular universities, the use of the common lands, the fraternity of the common creed.

I fear the professor will not follow me into matters so disturbing to his perfect picture of progress. But, in conclusion, there is one little question I should like to ask him, and it is this. If you cannot see Man, divine and democratic, under the disguises of all the centuries, why on earth should you suppose you will be able to see him under the disguises of all the nations and tribes? If the Dark Ages must be as dark as they look, why are the black men not so black as they are painted? If I may feel supercilious towards a Chaldean, why not towards a Chinaman? If I may despise a Roman for not having a steam-plough, why not a Russian for not wanting a steam-plough? If scientific industry is the supreme historical test, it divides us as much from backward peoples as from bygone peoples. It divides even European peoples from each other. And if that be the test, why bother to join the League of Nations Union?

G. K. CHESTERTON

THE EVOLUTION OF SLAVES

A very curious and interesting thing has recently happened in America. There has suddenly appeared an organized political attack on Darwinian Evolution, led by an old demagogue appealing entirely to the ideals of democracy. I mean no discredit to Mr. Bryan in calling him a demagogue; for I should have been far more heartily on his side in the days when he was a demagogue than in the days when he was a diplomatist. He was a much wiser man when he refused to allow the financiers to crucify humanity on a golden cross, than when he consented to allow the Kaiser to crucify it on an iron cross. The movement is religious and therefore popular; but it is Protestant and therefore provincial. Its opponents, the old guard of materialism, will of course do their best to represent it as something like the village that voted the earth was flat. But there is one sharp difference, which is the point of the whole position. If an ignorant man went about saying that the earth was flat, the scientific man would promptly and confidently answer, "Oh, nonsense; of course it's round." He might even condescend to give the real reasons, which I believe are quite different from the current ones. But when the private citizen rushes wild-eyed down the streets of Heliopolis, Neb., calling out "Have you heard the news? Darwin's wrong!" the scientific man does not say, "Oh, nonsense, of course he's right." He says tremulously, "Not entirely wrong; surely not entirely wrong"; and we can draw our conclusions. But I believe myself there is a deeper and more democratic force behind this reaction; and I think it worthy of further study.

I recently heard a debate on that American system of class privilege which we call for convenience Prohibition; and I was very much amused by one argument that was advanced in its favour. A very intelligent young American, a Rhodes scholar from Oxford, advanced the thesis that Prohibition was not a violation of liberty because, if it were fully established, its victims would never know what they had lost. If a generation of total abstainers could once grow up "without the desire" for drink, they would not be conscious of any restraint on their freedom. The argument is ingenious and promising and opens up a wide field of application. Thus, if I happen to find it convenient to keep miners or other proletarians permanently underground, I have only to make sure that all their babies are born in pitch darkness and they will certainly never imagine the light of day. My action therefore will not only be just and benevolent in itself, but will obviously involve not even the faintest infringement of the ideal of freedom. Or if I merely kidnap all the babies from all the mothers in the country, it is obvious that the infants will not remember their mothers, and in that sense will not miss them. There is therefore no reason why I

G. K. CHESTERTON

should not adopt this course; and even if I hide the babies from their mothers by locking them up in boxes, I shall not be violating the principle of liberty; because the babies will not understand what I have done. Or, to take a comparison even closer in many ways, there is an ordinary social problem like dress. I come to the conclusion that ladies spend too much money on dress, that it is a social evil because families suffer from the extravagance, and rivalries and seductions distract the state. I therefore decree, on the lines of Prohibitionist logic, that the law shall forbid anybody to wear any clothes at all. Nobody who grows up naked, according to this theory, will ever have any regrets for beauty or dignity or decency; and therefore will have suffered no loss. I cannot sufficiently express my admiration for the extraordinary simplicity which can smooth the path of Prussianism with this large, elementary and satisfactory principle. So long as we tyrannize enough we are not tyrannizing at all; and so long as we steal enough our victims will never know what has been stolen. Seriously, everybody knows that the rich planning the oppression of the poor will never lack a sycophant to act as a sophist. But I never dreamed that I should live to enjoy so crude and stark and startling a sophistry as this.

But the last example I gave, that of the normality of clothes or of nakedness, has a further relevance in this connexion. What is really at the back of the minds of the people who say these strange things is

one very simple error. They imagine that the drinking of fermented liquor has been an artifice and a
luxury; something odd like the strange self-indul-
gences praised by the decadent poets. This is simply
an accident of the ignorance of history and humanity. Drinking fermented liquor is not a fashion like
wearing a green carnation. It is a habit like wearing
clothes. It is one of the habits that are indeed man's
second nature; if indeed they are not his first nature.
Wine is purest and healthiest in the highest civilization, just as clothing is most complete in the highest civilization. But there is nothing to show that the
savage has not shed the clothes of a higher civilization, retaining only the ornaments; as a good many
fashionable people in our own civilization seem to be
doing now. And there is nothing to show that rud-
er races who brew their "native beers" in Africa or
Polynesia have not lost the art of brewing something
better; just as Prohibitionist America, before our
very eyes, has left off brewing Christian beer and
taken to drinking fermented wood-pulp and meth-
ylated spirit. The very example of modern America
falling from better to baser drinks, under a dismal
taboo, is a perfect model of the way in which civili-
zations have relapsed into savagery, and produced
the savages we know. But the point is that drink,
like dress, is the rule; and the exceptions only prove
the rule. There are individuals who for personal and
particular reasons are right to drink no liquor but
water; just as there are individuals who have to stay

G. K. CHESTERTON

in bed, and wear no clothes but bedclothes. There have been sects of Moslems and there have been sects of Adamites. There have been, as I have said, barbarized peoples fallen so far from civilization as to wear grotesque garments or none, or to drink bad beer or none. But nobody has ever seen Primitive Man, naked and drinking water; he is a myth of the modern mythologists. Man, as Aristotle saw long ago, is an abnormal animal whose nature it is to be civilized. In so far as he ever becomes uncivilized he becomes unnatural, and even artificial.

Now at the back of all this, of course, the real difference is religious. I only take this one case of what is called temperance for the sake of the wider philosophy that underlies it. When my young American friend talked of the next generation growing up without the desire for "alcohol," he had at the back of his mind a certain idea. It is the idea which I have just seen expressed by another American in a high-brow article, in the words: "Evolution does not stand still. We are not finished. The world is not finished." What it means is that the nature of man can be modified to suit the convenience of particular men; and this would certainly be very convenient. If the rich man wants the miners to live underground, he may really breed for it a new race as blind as bats and owls. If he finds it cheaper to run the schools and school inspections on Adamite principles, he can hope to produce Adamites not merely as a sect but as a species. And the same will be true of teetotalism or vegetarianism;

nature, having evolved man who is an ale-drinking animal, may now evolve a super-man, or a sub-man, who shall be a water-drinking animal. Having risen from a monkey who eats nuts to a man who eats mutton, he may rise yet higher by eating nuts again.

Thinking people, of course, know that all that is nonsense. They know there is no such constant flux of adaption. So far from saying that the evolution of man has not finished, they will point out that (as far as we know) it has not begun. In all the five thousand years of recorded history, and in all the prehistoric indications before it, there is not a shadow or suspicion of movement or change in the human biological type. Even evolution, let alone natural selection, is only a conjecture about things unknown, compared with the broad daylight of things known in all those thousands of years. The only difference is that evolution seems a probable conjecture, and natural selection is on the face of it an extravagantly improbable one. All this, which is obvious to thinking people, has at last become obvious even to the most unthinking; and *that* is the meaning of the attack on Darwinism in America and the battle of Mr. Bryan against the Missing Link. The secret is out. The obscurantism of the professors is over. Those of us who have humbly hammered on this point from time to time suddenly find ourselves hammering on an open door. For these changes almost always come suddenly; which is alone enough to show that human history at least has never been merely an evolution. As Darwinism

G. K. CHESTERTON

came with a rush, so Anti-Darwinism has come with a rush; and just as people who accepted evolution could not be held back from embracing natural selection, so it is likely enough that many, who now see reason to reject natural selection, will not be stopped in their course till they have also rejected evolution. They will merely have a vague but angry conviction that the professors have been kidding them, as they had before that the parsons had been kidding them. But behind all this there will be a very real moral and religious reaction; the meaning of which is what I have described in this article. It is the profound popular impression that scientific materialism, at the end of its hundred years, is found to have been used chiefly for the oppression of the people. Of this the most evident example is that evolution itself can be offered as something able to evolve a people who can be oppressed. As in the argument about Prohibition, it will offer to breed slaves; to produce a new race indifferent to its rights. Morally the argument is quite indistinguishable from justifying assassination by promising to bring up children as suicides, who will prefer to be poisoned.

IS DARWIN DEAD?

Mr. Ernest Newman, that lively and acute critic, once rebuked the arrogance of those of us who confessed that we knew nothing about music. Why he should suppose we are arrogant about it, if he does think so, I cannot quite understand. I, for one, am fully conscious of my inferiority to him and others through this deficiency; nor is it, alas, the only deficiency. I have sometimes thought it would be wholesome for anybody who has succeeded pretty well by some trick of some trade, to have a huge notice board or diagram hung in front of him all day; showing exactly where he stood in all the other crafts and competitions of mankind. Thus the poet's eye in a fine frenzy rolling, as it rose from the paper on which an entirely new type of villanelle had just sprung into being, would encounter the disconcerting facts and figures about his suitability to be a professional acrobat or a pearl-diver. On the other hand, the radiant victor in the great International Egg and Spoon Race can see at a glance how very far down he stands, so to speak, in the queue of those waiting for the post of Astronomer Royal. Most of us have at least one or two gaps in our general culture and information; and sometimes whole departments of knowledge are practically hidden from whole generations and classes of mankind. There is something very defective and disproportionate about even the ideal culture of a modern man. It may be that Mr. Newman is deeply read in that mediæval theology which is still the sub-conscious basis of most morality; but it is also possible that he is not. He may have at his fingers' ends that military art which has often turned the fortunes of history; but he may not. He would be none the less a highly cultivated gentleman, if he did not. Yet the mystical and the military mind have been at least as pivotal and practical in history as the musical mind. I can admire them all, but I have no claim to possess any of them.

But my ignorance of music happens to assist me with a convenient metaphor in the more controversial matter of my ignorance of science. I once made some remarks about the decline of Darwinism, in a review of the Wells "Outline of History." This aroused rather excited criticism; but one comparatively calm critic challenged what really interests me in the matter: he said that my conundrums about the wing of the bat and similar things "could easily be solved on purely Darwinian lines by any competent zoologist, or even by one so incompetent as myself." The conundrum in question, of course, concerns the survival value of features in their unfinished state. If a thing can fly it may survive, and if it has a wing it may fly; but if it cannot fly with half a wing, why should it survive with half a wing? Yet Darwinism pre-supposes that numberless generations could survive before one generation could fly. Now it is quite true that I am

G. K. CHESTERTON

not even an incompetent zoologist; and that my critic is more competent than I, if only in the mere fact of being a zoologist at all. Nevertheless, I adhere to my opinion, and do so for a reason that seems to me worthy of some little consideration. I do it because this does happen to be exactly one of those questions on which, as it seems to me, the independent critic has really a right to check the specialist. For it is a larger question of logic, and not a smaller question of fact. It is like the difficulty of believing that a half-penny can fall head or tail a hundred times running; which has nothing to do with the numismatic value of the coin. It is like the difficulty of believing that a mere tax could make a loaf cheaper, which has nothing to do with the agrarian craft of growing corn. There is a general tide of reason flowing against such improbabilities, even if they are possibilities; they would still be exceptions, and reason would be on the side of the rule. And whatever the details of natural history, this thing is against the very nature of things. To explain what I mean I will take this parallel of the technique of music, of which I know even less than of the technique of natural history. To begin with a simple though moving musical instrument, suppose an expert told me that a coach-horn could be blown quite as well if it were only two feet long. I should believe him; partly because it seems probable enough, and partly because I know nothing about the matter. I am not even an incompetent coach-horn blower. But I should certainly not believe him if he told me, as a generalization about all musical instruments, that half a musical instrument was better than no music, or even as good as any music. I should disbelieve it because it is inconsistent with the general nature of a musical instrument, or any instrument. I should disbelieve it long before I had thought of the thousand particular instruments to which it does not apply. I should not primarily need to think of the particular examples, though they are obvious enough. A stringed instrument cannot even be called stringed without two fixed points to hold both ends of the string. At the stage when the fiddle-strings floated like filaments in the void, feeling their way towards an evolutionary other end of nowhere, there could be nothing serving any purpose of a fiddle. A drum with a hole in is not a drum at all. But an evolutionary drum has to turn slowly into a drum, when it has begun by being only a hole. I cannot see any survival for a bagpipe that begins by being slit; I think such bagpipes would die with all their music in them. I feel a faint doubt, mingled with fascination, about the idea that a violin could grow out of the ground like a tree; it would at least make a charming fairy story. But whether or no a fiddle could grow like a tree, I feel sure nobody could play on it while it was still only a twig. But all these, as I say, are only examples that throng into the mind afterwards, of a principle seen in a flash from the first. Of things serving particular purposes, by a balance and arrangement of parts, it *cannot* be generally true that they are fit for use before they are finished for use. It is against the general nature of such things; and can only be true by an individual coincidence. I can see for myself, for instance, that some particular case like the trunk of an elephant might really be compared to the simpler case of the coach-horn. Length and flexibility *are* mere matters of degree; and I might possibly find it convenient if my nose were six inches longer, and sufficiently lively to be able to point right and left at various objects on the tea-table. But this is simply an accident of the particular qualities of length and laxity, not a general truth about the qualities of growth and use. It is not in the least true that I should experience the least convenience from the membrane between my fingers thickening or widening a little; even if an evolutionist at my elbow comforted and inspired me with the far-off divine event when my descendant should have the wings of a bat. Until the membrane can really be spread properly from point to point it is like the fiddle-string before it is stretched properly from point to point. It is no nearer serving its ultimate purpose than if it were not there at all. But it would be easy to find a similar animal parallel to the drum with a hole in it. There are monsters who would die instantly if they could not close the holes in their head under water. One supposes they would have died swiftly, before their closing apparatus could develop slowly. But the principle is a general one, and is involved in the very nature of any apparatus. It is only by way of figure of speech, in defence of the freedom of the ignorant, that I take the type of a musical apparatus. I take it because I am entirely ignorant of musical instruments. I am of the candid class of those who have "never tried" to perform on the violin. I cannot play upon this pipe; especially if it be a bagpipe. But if anybody tells me that the wildest pibroch rose from a whisper gradually, as a hole in the wind-bag was filled up gradually—why then I shall not be so rude, I hope, as to say that there is a windbag in his head, but I shall venture to say that there is a hole in his argument. And if he says that pieces of wood came together slowly, stick by stick, to form a fiddle, and that before it was yet a fiddle at all the sticks discoursed most excellent music—why, I fear I shall be content to say "fiddlesticks."

There is another answer often made which seems to me even more illogical. The critic generally says it is unreasonable to expect from the geological record that continuous gradation of types which the challengers of Darwinism demand. He says that only a part of the earth can be examined and that it could not in any case prove so much. This mode of argument involves an amazing oblivion of what is the thing to be proved, and who is trying to prove it. By hypothesis the Darwinians are trying to prove Darwinism. The Anti-Darwinians are not trying to prove anything; except that the Darwinians have not proved it. I do not demand anything, in the sense of complaining anything or the absence of anything.

　　　　　　　　　G. K. CHESTERTON

I am quite comfortable in a completely mysterious cosmos. I am not reviling the rocks or cursing the eternal hills for not containing these things. I am only saying that these are the things they would have to contain to make me believe something that somebody else wants me to believe. These traces are not things that the Anti-Darwinian demands. They are things that the Darwinian requires. The Darwinian requires them in order to convince his opponent of Darwinism; his opponent may be right or wrong, but he cannot be expected to accept the mere absence of them as proof of Darwinism. If the evidences in support of the theory are unfortunately hidden, why then we do not know whether they were in support of the theory. If the proofs of natural selection are lost, why then there are no proofs of natural selection; and there is an end of it.

And I would respectfully ask these critics what would be thought of a theological or miraculous argument which thus based itself on the very gaps in its own evidence. Let them indulge in the flight of fancy that I have just told them, let us say, that I saw the Devil at Brighton: and that the proof of his presence there can still be seen on the sands, in gigantic marks of a cloven hoof as big as the foot of an elephant. Suppose we all search the sands of Brighton and find no such thing. And suppose I then say that, after all, the tide might have washed away the footprints, or that the fiend may have flown through the air from his little country seat at the Dyke, or that he may have walked along the hard asphalt of Brighton parade, as proudly as once upon the flaming marl. To those acquainted with Brighton parade this will seem probable enough; but there would be a fallacy in merely saying that the evil spirit may have done all this. The sceptic will not unnaturally reply: "Yes, he may; and he may not; and it may be a legend; and you may be a liar; and I think our little investigation is now concluded." I am very far indeed from calling the Darwinian a liar; but I shall continue to say that he is not always a logician.

G. K. CHESTERTON

TURNING INSIDE OUT

When the author of "If Winter Comes" brought out another book about the life of the family, it was almost as much criticized as the first book was praised. I do not say that there was nothing to criticize, but I do say that I was not convinced by the abstract logic of the criticism. Probably the critics would have accepted it as a true story if the author had not been so incautious as to give it a true moral. And the moral is not fashionable in the press at the moment; for it is to the effect that a woman may gain a professional success at the price of a domestic failure. And it is the convention of journalism at this moment to support what is feminist against what is feminine. Anyhow, while the story might be criticized, the criticisms can certainly be criticized. It is not really conclusive to say that a woman may be ambitious in business without her children going to the bad. It is just as easy to say that a woman may be ambitious in politics without helping to murder an old gentleman in his bed. But that does not make "Macbeth" either inartistic or untrue. It is just as easy to say that a woman may be ambitious in society without tricking her husband into a debtor's prison, so that she may spend the time with a bald-headed nobleman with red whiskers. But that does not make the great scene in "Vanity Fair" unconvincing either in detail or design. The question in fiction is not whether that thing must occur, but whether that sort of thing may occur, and whether it is significant of larger things. Now this business of the woman at work and the woman at home is a very large thing, and this story about it is highly significant.

For in this matter the modern mind is inconsistent with itself. It has managed to get one of its rather crude ideals in flat contradiction to the other. People of the progressive sort are perpetually telling us that the hope of the world is in education. Education is everything. Nothing is so important as training the rising generation. Nothing is really important except the rising generation. They tell us this over and over again, with slight variations of the same formula, and never seem to see what it involves. For if there be any word of truth in all this talk about the education of the child, then there is certainly nothing but nonsense in nine-tenths of the talk about the emancipation of the woman. If education is the highest function in the State, why should anybody want to be emancipated from the highest function in the State? It is as if we talked of commuting the sentence that condemned a man to be President of the United States; or a reprieve coming in time to save him from being Pope. If education is the largest thing in the world, what is the sense of talking about a woman being liberated from the largest thing in the world? It is as if we were to rescue her from the cruel doom of being a poet like Shakespeare; or to pity

G. K. CHESTERTON

the limitations of an all-round artist like Leonardo da Vinci. Nor can there be any doubt that there is truth in this claim for education. Only precisely the sort of which it is particularly true is the sort called domestic education. Private education really is universal. Public education can be comparatively narrow. It would really be an exaggeration to say that the schoolmaster who takes his pupils in freehand drawing is training them in all the uses of freedom. It really would be fantastic to say that the harmless foreigner who instructs a class in French or German is talking with all the tongues of men and angels. But the mother dealing with her own daughters in her own home does literally have to deal with all forms of freedom, because she has to deal with all sides of a single human soul. She is obliged, if not to talk with the tongues of men and angels, at least to decide how much she shall talk about angels and how much about men.

In short, if education is really the larger matter, then certainly domestic life is the larger matter; and official or commercial life the lesser matter. It is a mere matter of arithmetic that anything taken from the larger matter will leave it less. It is a mere matter of simple subtraction that the mother must have less time for the family if she has more time for the factory. If education, ethical and cultural, really were a trivial and mechanical matter, the mother might possibly rattle through it as a rapid routine, before going about her more serious business of serving a capitalist for hire. If education were merely instruction, she might briefly instruct her babies in the multiplication tables, before she mounted to higher and nobler spheres as the servant of a Milk Trust or the secretary of a Drug Combine. But the moderns are perpetually assuring us that education is not instruction; they are perpetually insisting that it is not a mechanical exercise, and must on no account be an abbreviated exercise. It must go on at every hour. It must cover every subject. But if it must go on at all hours, it must not be neglected in business hours. And if the child is to be free to cover every subject, the parent must be free to cover every subject too.

For the idea of a non-parental substitute is simply an illusion of wealth. The advanced advocate of this inconsistent and infinite education for the child is generally thinking of the rich child; and all this particular sort of liberty should rather be called luxury. It is natural enough for a fashionable lady to leave her little daughter with the French governess or the Czecho-Slovakian governess or the Ancient Sanskrit governess, and know that one or other of these sides of the infant's intelligence is being developed; while she, the mother, figures in public as a money-lender or some other modern position of dignity. But among poorer people there cannot be five teachers to one pupil. Generally there are about fifty pupils to one teacher. There it is impossible to cut up the soul of a single child and distribute it among specialists. It is all we can do to tear in pieces the soul of a single schoolmaster, and distribute it in rags and scraps to a whole mob of boys. And even in the case of the wealthy child it is by no means clear that specialists are a substitute for spiritual authority. Even a millionaire can never be certain that he has not left out one governess, in the long procession of governesses perpetually passing under his marble portico; and the omission may be as fatal as that of the king who forgot to ask the bad fairy to the christening. The daughter, after a life of ruin and despair, may look back and say, "Had I but also had a Lithuanian governess, my fate as a diplomatist's wife in Eastern Europe would have been very different." But it seems rather more probable, on the whole, that what she would miss would not be one or other of these special accomplishments, but some commonsense code of morals or general view of life. The millionaire could, no doubt, hire a mahatma or mystical prophet to give his child a general philosophy. But I doubt if the philosophy would be very successful even for the rich child, and it would be quite impossible for the poor child. In the case of comparative poverty, which is the common lot of mankind, we come back to a general parental responsibility, which is the common sense of mankind. We come back to the parent as the person in charge of education. If you exalt the education, you must exalt the parental power with it. If you exaggerate the education, you must exaggerate the parental power with it. If you depreciate the parental power, you must depreciate education with it. If the young are always right and can do as they like, well and good; let us all be jolly, old and young, and free from every kind of responsibility. But in that case do not come pestering us with the importance of education, when nobody has any authority to educate anybody. Make up your mind whether you want unlimited education or unlimited emancipation, but do not be such a fool as to suppose you can have both at once.

There is evidence, as I have noted, that the more hard-headed people, even of the most progressive sort, are beginning to come back to realities in this respect. The new work of Mr. Hutchinson's is only one of many indications among the really independent intelligences, working on modern fiction, that the cruder culture of merely commercial emancipation is beginning to smell a little stale. The work of Miss Clemence Dane and even of Miss Sheila Kaye-Smith contains more than one suggestion of what I mean. People are no longer quite so certain that a woman's liberty consists of having a latch-key without a house. They are no longer wholly convinced that every housekeeper is dull and prosaic, while every bookkeeper is wild and poetical. And among the intelligent the reaction is actually strengthened by all the most modern excitements about psychology and hygiene. We cannot insist that every trick of nerves or train of thought is important enough to be searched for in libraries and laboratories, and not important enough for anybody to watch by simply staying at home. We cannot insist that the first

G. K. CHESTERTON

years of infancy are of supreme importance, and that mothers are not of supreme importance; or that motherhood is a topic of sufficient interest for men, but not of sufficient interest for mothers. Every word that is said about the tremendous importance of trivial nursery habits goes to prove that being a nurse is not trivial. All tends to the return of the simple truth that the private work is the great one and the public work the small. The human house is a paradox, for it is larger inside than out.

But in the problem of private versus public life there is another neglected truth. It is true of many masculine problems as well as of this feminine problem. Indeed, feminism falls here into exactly the same mistake as militarism and imperialism. I mean that anything on a grand scale gives the illusion of a grand success. Curiously enough, multiplication acts as a concealment. Repetition actually disguises failure. Take a particular man, and tell him to put on a particular kind of hat and coat and trousers, and to stand in particular attitudes in the back garden; and you will have great difficulty in persuading yourself (or him) that he has passed through a triumph and transfiguration. Order four hundred such hats, and eight hundred such trousers, and you will have turned the fancy costume into a uniform. Make all the four hundred men stand in the special attitudes on Salisbury Plain, and there will rise up before you the spirit of a regiment. Let the regiment march past, and, if you have any life in you above the brutes that perish, you will have an overwhelming sense that something splendid has just happened, or is just going to begin. I sympathize with this moral emotion in militarism; I think it does symbolize something great in the soul, which has given us the image of St. Michael. But I also realize that in practical relations that emotion can get mixed up with an illusion. It is not really possible to know the characters of all the four hundred men in the marching column as well as one might know the character of the one man attitudinizing in the back garden. If all the four hundred men were individual failures, we could still vaguely feel that the whole thing was a success. If we know the one man to be a failure, we cannot think him a success.

That is why a footman has become rather a foolish figure, while a foot-soldier remains rather a sublime one. Or rather, that is one of the reasons; for there are others much more worthy. Anyhow, footmen were only formidable or dignified when they could come in large numbers like foot-soldiers—when they were in fact the feudal army of some great local family, having some of the loyalty of local patriotism. Then a livery was as dignified as a uniform, because it really was a uniform. A man who said he served the Nevilles or rode with the Douglases could once feel much like a man fighting for France or England. But military feeling is mob feeling, noble as mob feeling may be. Parading one footman is like lunching on one pea, or curing baldness by the growth of one hair. There ought not to be anything but a plural

G. K. CHESTERTON

for flunkeys, any more than for measles or vermin or animalculæ or the sweets called hundreds and thousands. Strictly speaking, I suppose that a logical Latinist could say, "I have seen an animalcula"; but I never heard of a child having the moderation to remark, "I have eaten a hundred and thousand." Similarly, any one of us can feel that to have hundreds and thousands of slaves, let alone soldiers, might give a certain imaginative pleasure in magnificence. To have one slave reveals all the meanness of slavery. For the solitary flunkey really is the man in fancy dress, the man standing in the back-garden in the strange and the fantastic coat and breeches. His isolation reveals our illusion. We find our failure in the back-garden, when we have been dreaming a dream of success in the market-place. When you ride through the streets amid a great mob of vassals (you may have noticed) you have a genial and not ungenerous sense of being at one with them all. You cannot remember their names or count their numbers, but their very immensity seems a substitute for intimacy. That is what great men have felt at the head of great armies; and the reason why Napoleon or Foch would call his soldiers "*mes enfants.*" He feels at that moment that they are a part of him, as if he had a million arms and legs. But it is very different if you disband your army of lackeys; or if (as is, after all, possible) you have not got an army of lackeys. It is very different if you look at one lackey; one solitary solemn footman standing in your front hall. You never have the sense of being caught up into a rapture of unity with *him*. All your sense of social solidarity with your social inferiors has dropped from you. It is only in public that people can be so intimate as that. When you look into the eyes of the lonely footman, you see that his soul is far away.

In other words, you find yourself at the foot of a steep and staggering mountain crag, that is the real character and conscience of a man. To be really at one with that man, you would have to solve real problems and believe that your own solutions were real. In dealing with the one man you would really have a far huger and harder job than in dealing with your throng of thousands. And *that* is the job that people run away from when they wish to escape from domesticity to public work, especially educational work. They wish to escape from a sense of failure which is simply a sense of fact. They wish to recapture the illusion of the market-place. It is an illusion that departs in the dark interiors of domesticity, where the realities dwell. As I have said, I am very far from condemning it altogether; it is a lawful pleasure, and a part of life, in its proper proportion, like any other. But I am concerned to point out to the feminists and the faddists that it is not an approach to truth, but rather the opposite. Publicity is rather of the nature of a harmless romance. Public life at its very best will contain a great deal of harmless romancing, and much more often of very harmfulromancing. In other words, I am concerned with pointing out that the passage from private life to public life, while it may be right or wrong, or necessary or unnecessary, or desirable or undesirable, is always of necessity a passage from a greater work to a smaller one, and from a harder work to an easier one. And that is why most of the moderns do wish to pass from the great domestic task to the smaller and easier commercial one. They would rather provide the liveries of a hundred footmen than be bothered with the love-affairs of one. They would rather take the salutes of a hundred soldiers than try to save the soul of one. They would rather serve out income-tax papers or telegraph forms to a hundred men than meals, conversation, and moral support to one. They would rather arrange the educational course in history or geography, or correct the examination papers in algebra or trigonometry, for a hundred children, than struggle with the whole human character of one. For anyone who makes himself responsible for one small baby, as a whole, will soon find that he is wrestling with gigantic angels and demons.

In another way there is something of illusion, or of irresponsibility, about the purely public function, especially in the case of public education. The educationist generally deals with only one section of the pupil's mind. But he always deals with only one section of the pupil's life. The parent has to deal, not only with the whole of the child's character, but also with the whole of the child's career. The teacher sows the seed, but the parent reaps as well as sows. The schoolmaster sees more children, but it is not clear that he sees more childhood; certainly he sees less youth and no maturity. The number of little girls who take prussic acid is necessarily small. The boys who hang themselves on bed-posts, after a life of crime, are generally the minority. But the parent has to envisage the whole life of the individual, and not merely the school life of the scholar. It is not probable that the parent will exactly anticipate crime and prussic acid as the crown of the infant's career. But he will anticipate hearing of the crime if it is committed; he will probably be told of the suicide if it takes place. It is quite doubtful whether the schoolmaster or schoolmistress will ever hear of it at all. Everybody knows that teachers have a harassing and often heroic task, but it is not unfair to them to remember that in this sense they have an exceptionally happy task. The cynic would say that the teacher is happy in never seeing the results of his own teaching. I prefer to confine myself to saying that he has not the extra worry of having to estimate it from the other end. The teacher is seldom in at the death. To take a milder theatrical metaphor, he is seldom there on the night. But this is only one of many instances of the same truth: that what is called public life is not larger than private life, but smaller. What we call public life is a fragmentary affair of sections and seasons and impressions; it is only in private life that dwells the fullness of our life bodily.

STRIKES AND THE
SPIRIT OF WONDER

There is a story which pleases me so much that I feel sure I have repeated it in print, about an alleged and perhaps legendary lady secretary of Madam Blavatsky or Mrs. Besant, who was so much delighted with a new sofa or ottoman that she sat on it by preference when resting or reading her correspondence. At last it moved slightly, and she found it was a Mahatma covered with his Eastern robe and rigid in prayer, or some more impersonal ecstasy. That a lady secretary should have a seat any gentleman will approve; that a Mahatma should be sat on no Christian will deny; nevertheless, there is another possible moral to the fable which is a reproach rather to the sitter than the seat. It might be put, as in a sort of vision or allegory, by imagining that all our furniture really was made thus of living limbs instead of dead sticks. Suppose the legs of the table were literally legs—the legs of slaves standing still. Suppose the arms of an armchair really were arms—the arms of a patient domestic permanently held out, like those of an old nurse waiting for a baby. It would be calculated to make the luxurious occupant of the easy-chair feel rather like a baby; which might do him good. Suppose every sofa were like that of Mrs. Besant's secretary—simply made of a man. They need not be made merely of Theosophists or Buddhists—God forbid. Many of us would greatly prefer to trust ourselves to a Moslem or Turk. This might, with strict accuracy, be called sitting on an Ottoman. I have even read, I think, of some oriental potentate who rejoiced in a name sounding like "sofa." It might even be hinted that some of them might be Christians, but there is no reason, of course, why all of them should not be praying. To sit on a man while he was praying would doubtless require some confidence. It would also give a more literal version of the possession of a Prie-Dieu chair. It would be easy to expand the extravagance into a vision of a whole house alive, an architecture of arms and legs, a temple of temples of the spirit. The four walls might be made of men like the squares in military formation. There is even, perhaps, a shadow of the fantasy in the popular phrases that compare the roof to the human head, that name the chimney-pot hat after the chimney, or lightly allude to all modern masculine head-dresses as "tiles." But the only value of the vision, as of most visions— even the most topsy-turvy ones—is a moral value. It figures forth, in emblem and enigma, the truth that we do treat merely as furniture a number of people who are, at the very least, live stock. And the proof of it is that when they move we are startled like the secretary sitting on the praying man; but perhaps it is we who should begin to pray.

In the current criticisms of the Strikes there is a particular tone, which affects me not as a matter of politics, but rather of philosophy, or even of poetry. It

G. K. CHESTERTON

is, indeed, the servile spirit expressed, if not in its poetry, at least in its rhetoric. But it is a spirit I can honestly claim to have hated and done my best to hammer long before I ever heard of the Servile State, long before I ever dreamed of applying this test to Strikes, or indeed of applying it to any political question. I felt it originally touching things at once elemental and every day—things like grass or daylight, like stones or daisies. But in the light of it, at least, I always rebelled against the trend or tone of which I speak. It may roughly be described as the spirit of taking things for granted. But, indeed, oddly enough, the very form of this phrase rather misses its own meaning. The spirit I mean, strictly speaking, does not take things for granted. It takes them as if they had not been granted. It takes them as if it held them by something more autocratic than a right; by a cold and unconscious occupation, as stiff as a privilege and as baseless as a caprice. As a fact, things generally are granted, ultimately by God, but often immediately by men. But this type of man is so unconscious of what he has been given that he is almost unconscious of what he has got; not realizing things as gifts, he hardly realizes them as goods. About the natural things, with which I began, this oblivion has only inward and spiritual, and not outward and political, effects. If we forget the sun the sun will not forget us, or, rather, he will not remember us to revenge himself by "striking" at us with a sunstroke. The stars will not go on strike or extinguish the illumination of the universe as the electricians would extinguish the illumination of the city. And so, while we repeat that there is a special providence in a falling star, we can ignore it in a fixed star. But when we at once ignore and assume thousands of thinking, brooding, free, lonely and capricious human creatures, they will remind us that we can no more order souls than we can order stars. This primary duty of doubt and wonder has nothing to do with the rights or wrongs of special industrial quarrels. The workmen might be quite wrong to go on strike, and we should still be much more wrong in never expecting them to go on strike. Ultimately, it is a mystical but most necessary mood of astonishment at everything outside one's own soul—even one's own body. It may even involve a wild vision in which one's own boots on one's own feet seem to be things distant and unfamiliar. And if this sound a shade fantastic, it is far less fantastic than the opposite extreme—the state of the man who feels as if he owned not only his own feet, but hundreds of other human feet like a huge centipede, or as if he were a universal octopus, and all rails, tubes and tramlines were his own tentacles, the nerves of his own body, or the circulation of his own blood. That is a much worse nightmare, and at this moment a much commoner one.

Tennyson struck a true note of the nineteenth century when he talked about "the fairy-tales of science and the long result of time." The Victorians had a very real and even childlike wonder at things like the steam-engine or the telephone, considered as toys.

G. K. CHESTERTON

Unfortunately the long result of time, on the fairy-tales of science, has been to extend the science and lessen the fairy-tale, that is, the sense of the fairy-tale. Take for example the case of a strike on the Tubes. Suppose that at an age of innocence you had met a strange man who had promised to drive you by the force of the lightning through the bowels of the earth. Suppose he had offered, in a friendly way, to throw you from one end of London to the other, not only like a thunderbolt, but by the same force as a thunderbolt. Or if we picture it a pneumatic and not an electric railway; suppose he gaily promised to blow you through a pea-shooter to the other side of London Bridge. Suppose he indicated all these fascinating opportunities by pointing to a hole in the ground and telling you he would take you there in a sort of flying or falling room. I hope you would have agreed that there was a special providence in a falling room. But whether or no you could call it providential, you would agree to call it special. You would at least think that the strange man was a very strange man. You would perhaps call him a very strange and special liar, if he merely undertook to do it. You might even call him a magician, if he did do it. But the point is this, that you would not call him a Bolshevik merely because he did not do it. You would think it a wonderful thing that it should be done at all; passing in that swift car through those secret caverns, you would feel yourself whirled away like Cinderella carried off in the coach that had once been a pumpkin. But though such things happened in every fairy-tale, they were not expected in any fairy-tale. Nobody turned on the fairies and complained that they were not working, because they were not always working wonders. The press in those parts did not break into big headlines of "Pumpkins Held Up; No Transformation Scenes," or "Wands Won't Work; Famine of Coaches." They did not announce with horror a "Strike of Fairy Godmothers." They did not draw panic-stricken pictures of mobs of fairy godmothers, meeting in parks and squares, merely because the majority of pumpkins still continued to be pumpkins. Now I do not argue that we ought to treat every tube-girl as our fairy godmother; she might resent the familiarity, especially the suggestion of anything so near to a grandmother. But I do suggest that we should, by a return to earlier sentiments, realize that the tube servants are doing something for us that we could not do for ourselves; something that is no part of our natural capacities, or even of our natural rights. It is not inevitable, or in the nature of things, that when we have walked as we can or want to, somebody else should carry us further in a cart, even for hire: or that when we have wandered up a road and come to a river, a total stranger should take us over in a boat, even if we bribe him to do so. If we would look at things in this plain white daylight of wonder, that shines on all the roads of the fairy-tales, we come to see at last the simplest truth about the Strikes, which is utterly missed in all contemporary

G. K. CHESTERTON

comments on them. It is merely the fact that Strikers are not *doing* something: they are doing nothing. If you mean that they should be *made* to do something, say so, and establish slavery. But do not be muddled by the mere word "strike" into mixing it up with breaking a window or hitting a policeman on the nose. Do not be stunned by a metaphor; there are no metaphors in fairy-tales.

A NOTE ON OLD NONSENSE

The Suffragettes have found out that they were wrong; I might even be so egotistical as to say they have found out that we were right. At least they have found out that the modern plutocratic parliamentary franchise is what I for one always said it was. In other words, they are startled and infuriated to find that the most vital modern matters are not settled in Parliament at all, but mostly by a conflict or compromise between Trusts and Trade Unions. Hence Mrs. Flora Drummond actually cries aloud that she is being robbed of her precious vote; and says dramatically "We women are being disenfranchized"— apparently by "Soviets." It is as if somebody who had just spent half a million on a sham diamond, that ought never to have deceived anybody, should shriek from the window that thieves had stolen the real diamond that never existed at all.

Whether or no there are Soviets, there are undoubtedly Strikes; and I do not underrate the difficulty or danger of the hour. There is at least a case for blaming men for striking right and left, illogically and without a system; there is a case for blaming them for striking steadily and logically in accordance with a false system; there is a case for saying that "direct action" implies such a false system. But there is no case whatever for blaming them for having depreciated the waste paper of the Westminster ballot-box; for that was depreciated long before the war, and long before the word "Soviet" came to soothe and satisfy the mind of Mrs. Drummond. It is absurd to blame the poor miners for discrediting the members of Parliament, who could always be trusted to discredit themselves. It was not the wild destructive Soviet which decided that Parliament should not know who paid the bills of its own political parties; it was Parliament itself. It was not a mad Bolshevist addressing a mob who said that the men of the parliamentary group have to treat charges of corruption among themselves differently from those outside; it was the greatest living parliamentarian in a great parliamentary debate. Miners had no more to be with it than missionaries in the Cannibal Islands; it was not because men could not get coal that they wanted to get coronets; and the empty coal-scuttle did not fill the party chest. But in any case the policy of people like Mrs. Drummond seems to require explanation. I can only fall back on the suggestion I have already made; that she and her friends insisted on taking shares in a rotten concern. They were quite sincere; so far as anybody can be quite sincere who flatly refuses to listen to reason. They have no right to complain if those who had to listen to their lawlessness will not listen to their legalism.

As a fact such a lady is rather contemptuous than complaining. She says the miners do not want Nationalization; which may or may not be true. But she explains the demand by the old disdainful allusion to agitators; or Labour leaders who "have to beat the big drum or lose their jobs." Nobody of course could possibly connect Mrs. Flora Drummond with the idea of a big drum; any more than with a big horse or a uniform or a self-created military rank. But this particular school of Feminists must not be too fastidious in the present case. The miners are poor and rudely instructed men; and cannot be expected to have that touch of quiet persuasiveness and softening courtesy, by which the Militant Suffragettes did so much to defend the historic dignity of their sex. They have to fall back on something only too like a big drum, having no skill in the silvery flutings of the W.S.P.U., or that tender lute which Miss Pankhurst touched at twilight. But under all the disadvantages of the coarser sex, the advocates of Nationalization have not yet used all the methods that precedent might suggest to them. Mr. Smillie has not cut up any Raphaels or Rembrandts at the National Gallery; nor even set fire to any of the theatres he may happen to pass when he is out for a walk. Mr. Bonar Law, on returning home at evening, does not find Mr. Sidney Webb, a solitary figure chained to his railings. One of the Suffragettes distinguished herself by getting inside a grand piano; but it is seldom that we open our own private piano and find a large coal-miner inside the instrument. The coal-miner may be better at the big drum than the grand piano; but he remains on the outside of both; and his drum is really smaller than some. The big drum, however, is rather a convenient metaphor for something obvious and loud and hollow; and the true moral in the matter is that recent English history was a procession led far too much by the big drum; and the agitation about mere Parliamentary votes was one of the most recent and most remarkable examples of it.

What will be the future of the present industrial crisis I will not prophesy; but I do know that every element in the past, which has led to this impasse in the present, has been thus glorified as a mere novelty by such a noisy minority. It was just because sanguine and shallow people found it easier to act than to write, and easier to write than to think, that every one of the changes came which now complicate our position. The very industrialism which makes us dependent on coal, and therefore on coal-miners and coal-owners, was forced on us by fussy efficient fools, for whom anything fresh seemed to be free. Neither miners nor mine-owners could have put out the fire by which Shakespeare told his Winter's Tale. The unequal ownership, which has justly alienated the workers, was hurried happily through because the owners were new, and it did not matter that they were few. The blind hypocrisy with which our press and publicists hardened their hearts in the great strikes before the war, was made possible by loud evasions about political progress and especially by the big drum of Votes for Women. I have begun this essay on a controversial note, with the echo of an

G. K. CHESTERTON

old controversy; and yet I do not mean to be merely provocative. The Suffragettes are only doing what we all do; and I have only put them first as an example of accumulated abuses for which we are all responsible. I do not mean to blame the Suffragettes as they blame the Socialists; but only to point to an impasse of impenitence for which we are all to blame.

I am more and more convinced that what is wanted nowadays is not optimism or pessimism, but a sort of reform that might more truly be called repentance. The reform of a state ought to be a thing more like the reform of a thief, which involves the admission that he has been a thief. We ought not to be merely inventing consolations, or even merely prophesying disasters; we ought, first and foremost, to be confessing our own very bad mistakes. It is easy enough to say that the world is getting better, by some mysterious thing called progress—which seems to mean providence without purpose. But it is almost as easy to say the world is getting worse, if we assume that it is only the younger generation that has just begun to make it worse. It is easy enough to say that the country is going to the dogs, if we are careful to identify the dogs with the puppies. What we need is not the assertion that other people are going to the dogs, but the confession that we ourselves have only just come back from the swine. We also are the younger generation, in the sense of being the Prodigal Son. As somebody said, there is such a thing as the Prodigal Father. We could purchase hope at the dreadful price of humility. But all thinkers and writers, of all political parties and philosophical sects, seem to shrink from this notion of admitting they are on the wrong road and getting back on to the right one. They are always trying to pretend, by hook or crook, that they are all on the same somewhat meandering road, and that they were right in going east yesterday, though they are right in going west to-day. They will try to make out that every school of thought was an advance on the last school of thought, and that no apology is due to anybody. For instance, we might really have a moderate, cautious, and even conservative reform of the evils affecting Labour, if we would only confess that Capitalism itself was a blunder which it is very difficult to undo. As it is, men seem to be divided into those that think it an achievement so admirable that it cannot be improved upon, and those who think it an achievement so encouraging that it *can* be improved upon. The former will leave it in chaos, and the latter will probably improve it into slavery. Neither will admit what is the truth—that we have got to get *back* to a better distribution of property, as it was before we fell into the blunder of allowing property to be clotted into monstrous monopolies. For that involves admitting that we have made a mistake; and that we none of us have the moral courage to do.

I suggest very seriously that it will do good to our credit for courage and right reason if we drop this way of doing things. The conversions that have converted the world were not effected by this sort of

G. K. CHESTERTON

evolutionary curve. St. Paul did not pretend that he had changed slowly and imperceptibly from a Pharisee to a Christian. Victor Hugo did not maintain that he had been very right to be a Royalist, and only a little more right to be a Republican. If we have come to the conclusion that we have been wrong, let us say so, and congratulate ourselves on being now right; not insinuate that in some relative fashion we were just as right when we were wrong. For in this respect the progressive is the worst sort of conservative. He insists on conserving, in the most obstinate and obscurantist fashion, all the courses that have been marked out for progress in the past. He does literally, in the rather unlucky metaphor of Tennyson, "let the great world spin for ever down the ringing grooves of change." For anyone who changes in that fashion has only got into a groove. There is no obligation on anybody to invent evolutionary excuses for all these experiments. There is no need to be so much ashamed of our blunders as all that. It is human to err; and the only final and deadly error, among all our errors, is denying that we have ever erred.

MILTON AND MERRY ENGLAND

Mr. Freeman, in contributing to the "London Mercury" some of those critical analyses which we all admire, remarked about myself (along with compliments only too generous and strictures almost entirely just) that there was very little autobiography in my writings. I hope the reader will not have reason to curse him for this kindly provocation, watching me assume the graceful poses of Marie Bashkirtseff. But I feel tempted to plead it in extenuation or excuse for this article, which can hardly avoid being egotistical. For though it concerns one of those problems of literature, of philosophy and of history that certainly interest me more than my own psychology, it is one on which I can hardly explain myself without seeming to expose myself.

That valuable public servant, "The Gentleman with the Duster," has passed on from Downing Street, from polishing up the Mirrors and polishing off the Ministers, to a larger world of reflections in "The Glass of Fashion." I call the glass a world of reflections rather than a world of shadows; especially as I myself am one of those tenuous shades. And the matter which interests me here is that the critic in question complains that I have been very unjust to Puritans and Puritanism, and especially to a certain ethical idealism in them, which he declares to have been more essential than the Calvinism of which I "make so much." He puts the point in a genial but somewhat fantastic fashion by saying that the world owes something to the jokes of Mr. G. K. Chesterton, but more to the moral earnestness of John Milton. This involves rather a dizzy elevation than a salutary depression; and the comparison is rather too overwhelming to be crushing. For I suppose the graceful duster of mirrors himself would hardly feel crushed, if I told him he did not hold the mirror up to Nature quite so successfully as Shakespeare. Nor can I be described as exactly reeling from the shock of being informed that I am a less historic figure than Milton. I know not how to answer, unless it be in the noble words of Sam Weller: "That's what we call a self-evident proposition, as the cats'-meat-man said to the housemaid when she said he was no gentleman." But for all that I have a controversial issue with the critic about the moral earnestness of Milton, and I have a confession to make which will seem to many only too much in the personal manner referred to by Mr. Freeman.

My first impulse to write, and almost my first impulse to think, was a revolt of disgust with the Decadents and the æsthetic pessimism of the 'nineties. It is now almost impossible to bring home to anybody, even to myself, how final that *fin de siècle* seemed to be; not the end of the century but the end of the world. To a boy his first hatred is almost as immortal as his first love. He does not realize that the objects

G. K. CHESTERTON

of either can alter; and I did not know that the twilight of the gods was only a mood. I thought that
all the wit and wisdom in the world was banded together to slander and depress the world, and in becoming an optimist I had the feelings of an outlaw.
Like Prince Florizel of Bohemia, I felt myself to be
alone in a luxurious Suicide Club. But even the death
seemed to be a living or rather everlasting death. To-
day the whole thing is merely dead; it was not sufficiently immortal to be damned. But then the image
of Dorian Gray was really an idol, with something
of the endless youth of a god. To-day the picture of
Dorian Gray has really grown old. Dodo then was
not merely an amusing female; she was the eternal
feminine. To-day the Dodo is extinct. Then, above
all, everyone claiming intelligence insisted on what
was called "Art for art's sake." To-day even the biog-
rapher of Oscar Wilde proposes to abandon "art for
art's sake," and to substitute "art for life's sake." But
at the time I was more inclined to substitute "no art,
for God's sake." I would rather have had no art at all
than one which occupies itself in matching shades
of peacock and turquoise for a decorative scheme of
blue devils. I started to think it out, and the more I
thought of it the more certain I grew that the whole
thing was a fallacy; that art could not exist apart
from, still less in opposition to, life; especially the
life of the soul, which is salvation; and that great art
never had been so much detached as that from conscience and common sense, or from what my critic

would call moral earnestness. Unfortunately, by the time I had exposed it as a fallacy, it had entirely evaporated as a fashion. Since then I have taken universal annihilations more lightly. But I can still be stirred, as man always can be by memories of their first excitements or ambitions, by anything that shows the cloven hoof of that particular blue devil. I am still ready to knock him about, though I no longer think he has a cloven hoof or even a lame leg to stand on. But for all that there is one real argument which I still recognize on his side; and that argument is in a single word. There is still one word which the æsthete can whisper; and the whisper will bring back all my childish fears that the æsthete may be right after all. There is one name that does seem to me a strong argument for the decadent doctrine that "art is unmoral." When that name is uttered, the world of Wilde and Whistler comes back with all its cold levity and cynical connoisseurship. The butterfly becomes a burden and the green carnation flourishes like the green bay-tree. For the moment I do believe in "art for art's sake." And that name is John Milton.

It does really seem to me that Milton was an artist, and nothing but an artist; and yet so great an artist as to sustain by his own strength the idea that art can exist alone. He seems to me an almost solitary example of a man of magnificent genius whose greatness does not depend at all upon moral earnestness, or upon anything connected with morality. His greatness is in a style, and a style which seems to me

G. K. CHESTERTON

rather unusually separate from its substance. What is the exact nature of the pleasure which I, for one, take in reading and repeating some such lines, for instance, as those familiar ones:

Dying put on the weeds of Dominic
Or in Franciscan think to pass disguised.

So far as I can see, the whole effect is in a certain unexpected order and arrangement of words, independent and distinguished, like the perfect manners of an eccentric gentleman. Say instead "Put on in death the weeds of Dominic," and the whole unique dignity of the line has broken down. It is something in the quiet but confident inversion of "Dying put on" which exactly achieves that perpetual slight novelty which Aristotle profoundly said was the language of poetry. The idea itself is at best an obvious and even conventional condemnation of superstition, and in the ultimate sense a rather superficial one. Coming where it does, indeed, it does not so much suggest moral earnestness as rather a moralizing priggishness. For it is dragged in very laboriously into the very last place where it is wanted, before a splendidly large and luminous vision of the world newly created, and the first innocence of earth and sky. It is that passage in which the wanderer through space approaches Eden; one of the most unquestionable triumphs of all human literature. That one book at least of "Paradise Lost" could claim the more audacious title of "Paradise Found." But if it was necessary for the poet going to Eden to pass through Limbo, why was it necessary to pass through Lambeth and Little Bethel? Why should he go there viâ Rome and Geneva? Why was it necessary to compare the débris of Limbo to the details of ecclesiastical quarrels in the seventeenth century, when he was moving in a world before the dawn of all the centuries, or the shadow of the first quarrel? Why did he talk as if the Church was reformed before the world was made, or as if Latimer lit his candle before God made the sun and moon? Matthew Arnold made fun of those who claimed divine sanction for episcopacy by suggesting that when God said "Let there be light," He also said "Let there be Bishops." But his own favourite Milton went very near suggesting that when God said "Let there be light," He soon afterwards remarked "Let there be Nonconformists." I do not feel this merely because my own religious sympathies happen to be rather on the other side. It is indeed probable that Milton did not appreciate a whole world of ideas in which he saw merely the corruptions: the idea of relics and symbolic acts and the drama of the death-bed. It does not enlarge his place in the philosophy of history that this should be his only relation either to the divine demagogy of the Dogs of God or to the fantastical fraternity of the Jugglers of God. But I should feel exactly the same incongruity if the theological animus were the other way. It would be equally disproportionate if the approach to Eden

G. K. CHESTERTON

were interrupted with jokes against Puritans, or if Limbo were littered with steeple-crowned hats and the scrolls of interminable Calvinistic sermons. We should still feel that a book of "Paradise Lost" was not the right place for a passage from Hudibras. So far from being morally earnest, in the best sense, there is something almost philosophically frivolous in the incapacity to think firmly and magnanimously about the First Things, and the primary colours of the creative palette, without spoiling the picture with this ink-slinging of sectarian politics. Speaking from the standpoint of moral earnestness, I confess it seems to me trivial and spiteful and even a little vulgar. After which impertinent criticism, I will now repeat in a loud voice, and for the mere lust of saying it as often as possible:

Dying put on the weeds of Dominic
Or in Franciscan think to pass disguised.

And the exuberant joy I take in it is the nearest thing I have ever known to art for art's sake.

In short, it seems to me that Milton was a great artist, and that he was also a great accident. It was rather in the same sense that his master Cromwell was a great accident. It is not true that all the moral virtues were crystallized in Milton and his Puritans. It is not true that all the military virtues were concentrated in Cromwell and his Ironsides. There were masses of moral devotion on the other side, and masses of military valour on the other side. But it did so happen that Milton had more ability and success in literary expression, and Cromwell more ability and success in military science, than any of their many rivals. To represent Cromwell as a fiend or Milton as a hypocrite is to rush to another extreme and be ridiculous; they both believed sincerely enough in certain moral ideas of their time. Only they were not, as seems to be supposed, the only moral ideas of their time. And they were not, in my private opinion, the best moral ideas of their time. One of them was the idea that wisdom is more or less weakened by laughter and a popular taste in pleasure; and we may call this moral earnestness if we like. But the point is that Cromwell did not succeed by his moral earnestness, but by his strategy; and Milton did not succeed by his moral earnestness, but by his style. And, first of all, let me touch on the highest form of moral earnestness and the relation of Milton to the religious poetry of his day. "Paradise Lost" is certainly a religious poem; but, for many of its admirers, the religion is the least admirable part of it. The poet professes indeed to justify the ways of God to men; but I never heard of any men who read it in order to have them justified, as men do still read a really religious poem, like the dark and almost sceptical Book of Job. A poem can hardly be said to justify the ways of God, when its most frequent effect is admittedly to make people sympathize with Satan. In all this I am in a sense arguing against myself; for all my instincts, as

G. K. CHESTERTON

I have said, are against the æsthetic theory that art so great can be wholly irreligious. And I agree that even in Milton there are gleams of Christianity. Nobody quite without them could have written the single line: "By the dear might of Him that walked the waves." But it is hardly too much to say that it is the one place where that Figure walks in the whole world of Milton. Nobody, I imagine, has ever been able to recognize Christ in the cold conqueror who drives a chariot in the war in heaven, like Apollo warring on the Titans. Nobody has ever heard Him in the stately disquisitions either of the Council in Heaven or of Paradise Regained. But, apart from all these particular problems, it is surely the general truth that the great religious epic strikes us with a sense of disproportion; the sense of how little it is religious considering how manifestly it is great. It seems almost strange that a man should have written so much and so well without stumbling on Christian tradition.

Now in the age of Milton there was a riot of religious poetry. Most of it had moral earnestness, and much of it had splendid spiritual conviction. But most of it was not the poetry of the Puritans; on the contrary, it was mostly the poetry of the Cavaliers. The most real religion—we might say the most realistic religion—is not to be found in Milton, but in Vaughan, in Treherne, in Crashaw, in Herbert, and even in Herrick. The best proof of it is that the religion is alive to-day, as religion and not merely as literature. A Roman Catholic can read Crashaw, an

Anglo-Catholic can read Herbert, in a direct devotional spirit; I gravely doubt whether many modern Congregationalists read the theology of "Paradise Lost" in that spirit. For the moment I mention only this purely religious emotion; I do not deny that Milton's poetry, like all great poetry, can awaken other great emotions. For instance, a man bereaved by one of the tragedies of the Great War might well find a stoical serenity in the great lines beginning "Nothing is here for tears." That sort of consolation is uttered, as nobly as it could be uttered, by Milton; but it might be uttered by Sophocles or Goethe, or even by Lucretius or Voltaire. But supposing that a man were seeking a more Christian kind of consolation, he would not find it in Milton at all, as he would find it in the lines beginning "They are all gone into the world of light." The whole of the two great Puritan epics do not contain all that is said in saying "O holy hope and high humility." Neither hope nor humility were Puritan specialities.

But it was not only in devotional mysticism that these Cavaliers could challenge the great Puritan; it was in a mysticism more humanistic and even more modern. They shine with that white mystery of daylight which many suppose to have dawned with Wordsworth and with Blake. In that sense they make earth mystical where Milton only made heaven material. Nor are they inferior in philosophic freedom; the single line of Crashaw, addressed to a woman, "By thy large draughts of intellectual day," is less likely, I

G. K. CHESTERTON

fancy, to have been addressed by Adam to Eve, or by Milton to Mrs. Milton. It seems to me that these men were superior to Milton in magnanimity, in chivalry, in joy of life, in the balance of sanity and subtlety, in everything except the fact (not wholly remote from literary criticism) that they did not write so well as he did. But they wrote well enough to lift the load of materialism from the English name; and show us the shining fields of a paradise that is not wholly lost.

Of such was the Anti-Puritan party; and the reader may learn more about it from the author of "The Glass of Fashion." There he may form a general idea of how, but for the Puritans, England would have been abandoned to mere ribaldry and licence; blasted by the blasphemies of George Herbert; rolled in the mire of the vile materialism of Vaughan; tickled to ribald laughter by the cheap cynicism and taproom familiarities of Crashaw and Treherne. But the same Cavalier tradition continued into the next age, and indeed into the next century; and the critic must extend his condemnation to include the brutal buffooneries of Bishop Ken or the gay and careless worldliness of Jeremy Collier. Nay, he must extend it to cover the last Tories who kept the tradition of the Jacobites; the careless merriment of Dean Swift, the godless dissipation of Dr. Johnson. None of these men were Puritans; all of them were strong opponents of political and religious Puritanism. The truth is that English literature bears a very continuous and splendid testimony to the fact that England was not merely Puritan. Ben Jonson in "Bartholomew Fair" spoke for most English people, and certainly for most English poets. Anti-Puritanism was the one thing common to Shakespeare and Dryden, to Swift and Johnson, to Cobbett and Dickens. And the historical bias the other way has come, not from Puritan superiority, but simply from Puritan success. It was the political triumph of the party, in the Revolution and the resultant commercial industrialism, that suppressed the testimony of the populace and the poets. Loyalty died away in a few popular songs; the Cromwellians never had any popular song to die. English history has moved away from English literature. Our culture, like our agriculture, is at once very native and very neglected. And as this neglect is regrettable, if only as neglect of literature, I will pause in conclusion upon the later period, two generations after Milton, when the last of the true Tories drank wine with Bolingbroke or tea with Johnson.

The truth that is missed about the Tories of this tradition is that they were rebels. They had the virtues of rebels; they also had the vices of rebels. Swift had the fury of a rebel; Johnson the surliness of a rebel; Goldsmith the morbid sensibility of a rebel; and Scott, at the end of the process, something of the despair and mere retrospection of a defeated rebel. And the Whig school of literary criticism, like the Whig school of political history, has omitted or missed this truth about them, because it necessarily omitted the very existence of the thing against which they rebelled.

G. K. CHESTERTON

For Macaulay and Thackeray and the average of Victorian liberality the Revolution of 1688 was simply an emancipation, the defeat of the Stuarts was simply a downfall of tyranny and superstition; the politics of the eighteenth century were simply a progress leading up to the pure and happy politics of the nineteenth century; freedom slowly broadening down, etc., etc. This makes the attitude of the Tory rebels entirely meaningless; so that the critics in question have been forced to represent some of the greatest Englishmen who ever lived as a mere procession of lunatics and ludicrous eccentrics. But these rebels, right or wrong, can only be understood in relation to the real power against which they were rebelling; and their titanic figures can best be traced in the light of the lightning which they defied. That power was a positive thing; it was anything but a mere negative emancipation of everybody. It was as definite as the monarchy which it had replaced; for it was an aristocracy that replaced it. It was the oligarchy of the great Whig families, a very close corporation indeed, having Parliament for its legal form, but the new wealth for its essential substance. That is why these lingering Jacobites appear most picturesque when they are pitted against some of the princes of the new aristocratic order. That is why Bolingbroke remains in the memory, standing in his box at the performance of "Cato," and flinging forth his defiance to Marlborough. That is why Johnson remains rigid in his magnificent disdain, hurling his defiance at Chesterfield. Churchill and Chesterfield were not small men, either in personality or in power; they were brilliant ornaments of the triumph of the world. They represented the English governing class when it could really govern; the modern plutocracy when it still deserved to be called an aristocracy also. And the whole point of the position of these men of letters is that they were denying and denouncing something which was growing every day in prestige and prosperity; which seemed to have, and indeed had, not only the present but the future on its side. The only thing it had not got on its side was the ancient tradition of the English populace. That populace was being more and more harried by evictions and enclosures, that its old common lands and yeoman freeholds might be added to the enormous estates of the all-powerful aristocracy. One of the Tory rebels has himself made that infamy immortal in the great lines of the "Deserted Village." At least, it is immortal in the sense that it can never now be lost for lovers of English literature; but even this record was for a long time lost to the public by under-valuation and neglect. In recent times the "Deserted Village" was very much of a deserted poem. But of that I may have occasion to speak later. The point for the moment is that the psychology of these men, in its evil as well as its good, is to be interpreted not so much in terms of a lingering loyalty as of a frustrated revolution. Some of them had, of course, elements of extravagance and morbidity peculiar to their own characters; but they grew ten times more extravagant and more morbid as

G. K. CHESTERTON

their souls swelled within them at the success of the shameless and the insolence of the fortunate. I doubt whether anybody ever felt so bitter against the Stuarts. Now this misunderstanding has made a very regrettable gap in literary criticism. The masterpieces of these men are represented as much more crabbed or cranky or inconsequent than they really were, because their objective is not seen objectively. It is like judging the raving of some Puritan preacher without allowing for the fact that the Pope or the King had ever possessed any power at all. To ignore the fact of the great Whig families because of the legal fiction of a free Parliament is like ignoring the feelings of the Christian martyrs about Nero, because of the legal fiction that the Imperator was only a military general. These fictions do not prevent imaginative persons from writing books like the "Apocalypse" or books like "Gulliver's Travels."

I will take only one example of what I mean by this purely literary misunderstanding: an example from "Gulliver's Travels" itself. The case of the under-valuation of Swift is a particularly subtle one, for Swift was really unbalanced as an individual, which has made it much easier for critics not to keep the rather delicate balance of justice about him. There is a superficial case for saying he was mad, apart from the physical accident of his madness; but the point is that even those who have realized that he was sometimes mad with rage have not realized what he was in a rage with. And there is a curious illustration of this in the conclusion of the story of Gulliver. Everyone remembers the ugly business about the Yahoos, and the still uglier business about the real human beings who reminded the returned traveller of Yahoos; how Gulliver shrank at first from his friends, and would only gradually consent to sit near his wife. And everybody remembers the picturesque but hostile sketch which Thackeray gives of the satire and the satirist; of Swift as the black and evil blasphemer sitting down to write his terrible allegory, of which the only moral is that all things are, and always must be, valueless and vile. I say that everybody remembers both these literary passages; but, indeed, I fear that many remember the critical who do not really remember the creative passage, and that many have read Thackeray who have not read Swift.

Now it is here that purely literary criticism has a word to say. A man of letters may be mad or sane in his cerebral constitution; he may be right or wrong in his political antipathies; he may be anything we happen to like or dislike from our own individual standpoint. But there is one thing to which a man of letters has a right, whatever he is, and that is a fair critical comprehension of any particular literary effect which he obviously aims at and achieves. He has a right to his climax, and a right not to be judged without reference to his climax. It would not be fair to leave out the beautiful last lines of "Paradise Lost" as mere bathos; without realizing that the poet had a fine intention in allowing that conclusion, after all

G. K. CHESTERTON

the thunder and the trumps of doom, to fall and fade away on a milder note of mercy and reasonable hope. It would not be fair to stigmatize the incident of Ignorance, damned at the very doors of heaven at the end of Bunyan's book, as a mere blot of black Calvinist cruelty and spite, without realizing that the writer fully intended its fearful irony, like a last touch of the finger of fear. But this justice which is done to the Puritan masters of imagination has hardly been done to the great Tory master of irony. No critic I have read has noticed the real point and climax of that passage about the Yahoos. Swift leads up to it ruthlessly enough, for an artist of that sort is often ruthless; and it is increased by his natural talent for a sort of mad reality of detail, as in his description of the slowly diminished distance between himself and his wife at the dinner-table. But he was working up to something that he really wished to say, something which was well worth saying, but which few seem to have thought worth hearing. He suggests that he gradually lost the loathing for humanity with which the Yahoo parallel had inspired him, that although men are in many ways petty and animal, he came to feel them to be normal and tolerable; that the sense of their unworthiness now very seldom returns; and indeed that there is only one thing that revives it. If one of these creatures exhibits Pride— —.

That is the voice of Swift, and the cry arraigning aristocracy. It is natural for a monkey to collect nuts, and it may be pardonable for John Churchill to collect guineas. But to think that John Churchill can be proud of his heap of guineas, can convert them into stars and coronets, and can carry that calm and classic face disdainful above the multitude! It is natural for she-monkeys to be mated somehow; but to think that the Duchess of Yarmouth is proud of being the Duchess of Yarmouth! It may not be surprising that the nobility should have scrambled like screaming Yahoos for the rags and ribbons of the Revolution, tripping up and betraying anybody and everybody in turn, with every dirty trick of treason, for anything and everything they could get. But that those of them who had got everything should then despise those who had got nothing, that the rich should sneer at the poor for having no part of the plunder, that this oligarchy of Yahoos should actually feel superior to anything or anybody—that does move the prophet of the losing side to an indignation which is something much deeper and nobler than the negative flippancies that we call blasphemy. Swift was perhaps more of a Jeremiah than an Isaiah, and a faulty Jeremiah at that; but in this great climax of his grim satire he is none the less a seer and a speaker of the things of God; because he gives the testimony of the strongest and most searching of human intellects to the profound truth of the meanness and imbecility of pride.

And the other men of the same tradition had essentially the same instinct. Johnson was in many ways unjust to Swift, just as Cobbett was afterwards unjust to Johnson. But looking back up the perspective

G. K. CHESTERTON

of history we can all see that those three great men were all facing the same way; that they all regretted the rise of a rapacious and paganized commercial aristocracy, and its conquest over the old popular traditions, which some would call popular prejudices. When Johnson said that the devil was the first Whig, he might have merely varied the phrase by saying that he was the first aristocrat. For the men of this Tory tradition, in spirit if not in definition, distinguished between the privilege of monarchy and that of the new aristocracy by a very tenable test. The mark of aristocracy is ambition. The king cannot be ambitious. We might put it now by saying that monarchy is authority; but in its essence aristocracy is always anarchy. But the men of that school did not criticize the oligarch merely as a rebel against those above; they were well aware of his activities as an oppressor of those below. This aspect, as has already been noted, was best described by a friend of Johnson, for whom Johnson had a very noble and rather unique appreciation—Oliver Goldsmith.

A recent and sympathetic critic in the *Mercury* used the phrase that Mr. Belloc had been anticipated by Disraeli in his view of England as having evolved into a Venetian oligarchy. The truth is that Disraeli was anticipated by Bolingbroke and the many highly intelligent men who agreed with him; and not least by Goldsmith. The whole view, including the very parallel with Venice, can be found stated with luminous logic and cogency in the "Vicar of Wakefield."

And Goldsmith attacked the problem entirely from the popular side. Nobody can mistake his Toryism for a snobbish submission to a privilege or title:

> Princes and lords, the shadow of a shade,
> A breath can make them, as a breath has made:
> But a bold peasantry, a nation's pride,
> When once destroyed can never be supplied.

I hope he was wrong; but I sometimes have a horrible feeling that he may have been right.

But I have here, thank God, no cause for touching upon modern politics. I was educated, as much as my critic, in the belief that Whiggism was a pure deliverance; and I hope I am still as willing as he to respect Puritans for their individual virtue as well as for their individual genius. But it moves all my memories of the unmorality of the 'nineties to be charged with indifference to the importance of being earnest. And it is for the sake of English literature that I protest against the suggestion that we had no purity except Puritanism, or that only a man like the author of "Paradise Lost" could manage to be on the side of the angels.

* * *

On Peace Day I set up outside my house two torches, and twined them with laurel; because I thought at least there was nothing pacifist about laurel. But that night, after the bonfire and the fireworks had faded, a wind grew and blew with gathering violence, blowing away the rain. And in the morning I found one of the laurelled posts torn off and lying at random on the rainy ground; while the other still stood erect, green and glittering in the sun. I thought that the pagans would certainly have called it an omen; and it was one that strangely fitted my own sense of some great work half fulfilled and half frustrated. And I thought vaguely of that man in Virgil, who prayed that he might slay his foe and return to his country; and the gods heard half the prayer, and the other half was scattered to the winds. For I knew we were right to rejoice; since the tyrant was indeed slain and his tyranny fallen for ever; but I know not when we shall find our way back to our own land.